The Dynamics of Small Groups
Within the Church

The Dynamics
of Small Groups
Within the Church

by
Bill Vaughn

BEACON HILL PRESS OF KANSAS CITY
Kansas City, Missouri

Copyright 1980
Beacon Hill Press of Kansas City

ISBN: 0-8341-0672-8

Printed in the
United States of America

Permission to quote from the following copyrighted versions of the Bible is acknowledged with appreciation:

The *Revised Standard Version of the Bible* (RSV), copyrighted 1946, 1952, © 1971, 1973.

The *New Testament in Modern English* (Phillips). Revised Edition © J. B. Phillips 1958, 1960, 1972. By permission of the Macmillan Publishing Co., Inc.

The Living Bible (TLB), © 1971 by Tyndale House Publishers, Wheaton, Ill.

Dedication

To Ruth

Who "lights up my life"
with her limitless capacity
for love

Contents

Contents

Preface

A universal of human experience is captured in these words of Paul:

"We are pressed on every side by troubles. . . . We are perplexed because we don't know why things happen as they do . . . We are hunted down . . . We get knocked down" (2 Cor. 4:8-9, TLB).

How the heart, then, yearns for
      someone to share with
      someone to bear with
      someone to *care!*
God responds to this universal need with this solution:
"I will welcome you, and be a Father to you,
and you will be my sons and daughters" (2 Cor. 6:17-18, TLB).
"'Come and talk with me,
O my people.'
And my heart responds,

'Lord, I am coming'" (Ps. 27:8, TLB).
"I was helpless in the hand of God,
and when he said to me,
'Go out into the valley and I will talk to you there'
I arose and went, and oh, I saw
the glory of the Lord there" (Ezek. 3:22-23, TLB).

9

When the "sons and daughters" of the Father God gather together in small groups where they may
> share with,
> bear with,
> care about each other

on an interpersonal basis with the Heavenly Father who said, "Go [into the house] . . . and I will talk to you there," these divine-family members can see the "glory of the Lord there" as in no other place, in no other way.

The fellowship of the whole Body of Christ in the sanctuary is vital, but no more so than the coming of "two or three . . . in my name" who can best work together as *family* . . .
> sharing with
> bearing with
> caring!

Go ye into all the world, and preach the gospel to every creature (Mark 16:15).

This Great Commission applies to the far-flung-corners-of-the-globe people. It also applies to your neighbor next door. The purpose of the small group within the church is to meet the universal heart needs of "sons and daughters" already reborn into the family of God. But it is more. Its purpose is to include every neighbor, friend, and acquaintance within your sphere in the invitation to become "born again" into a saving relationship with the Father God, to learn of Him, and to "go" to your house where they feel comfortable; and God, through His Spirit, and through you, His human channel, will "talk to [them] there."

You know many people who would never consider your invitation to go to the church sanctuary. There are too many barriers built into their background—training, culture, whatever. But many of these people are *aching* to know more of God *somehow*. And they would be glad to come to your known, familiar house once a week, to learn with you and a few others how better to be open to hearing God's voice calling people to himself in salvation, providing answers to the personal agonies, dilemmas, and frustrations which pulsate through their lives.

Such is the rationale behind the organization of small groups within the church.

The small group within the church
        Is
        a
        God-instrument
        that
        helps
        each
        member
        toward
        God's
        goal
        of
        Christlikeness
        in
        inner
        spirit
        and in one's total outer behavior.

The small group within the church
        Is
        a
        God-instrument
        that
        encourages
        each
        member

to
grow
in
Christian characteristics
and toward his fullest potential as a useful
person in the world community.

The small group within the church
Is
a
God-instrument
that
challenges
each
member
to
reach
one
hand
up
to
God
and the other hand in loving outreach to
all one's fellowmen.

The small group is ministry!

—Bill Vaughn

Acknowledgments

Permission to quote from copyrighted material is gratefully acknowledged, as follows:

Wm. C. Brown Company: John K. Brilhart, *Effective Group Discussion*, 2nd ed., © 1974; 3rd ed., © 1967, 1974, 1978. Robert S. Cathcart and Larry A. Samovar, *Small Group Communication: A Reader*, © 1974, 1979.

Harper and Row, Publishers, Inc., 10 East 53rd St., New York: Irving Lee, *How to Talk with People*, 1952.

Holt, Rinehart, and Winston: David Berlo, *The Process of Communication: An Introduction to Theory and Practice*, copyright © 1960. Halbert E. Gulley, *Discussion, Conference, and Group Process*. Second ed., © 1960, 1968.

Houghton Mifflin Company: Thomas Gordon, *Group-centered Leadership: A Way of Releasing the Creative Power of Groups*, copyright © 1965 by Thomas Gordon.

Richard D. Irwin, Inc.: William Haney, *Communication and Organizational Behavior: Text and Cases*, 3rd ed., © 1973.

Mayfield Publishing Company: Joseph Luft, *Group Processes: An Introduction to Group Dynamics*, copyright © 1963, 1970, by Joseph Luft.

Prentice-Hall, Inc.: Jane Blankenship, *Public Speaking: A Rhetorical Perspective*, 2nd ed., 1972.

Random House: Lewis Carroll, *Alice's Adventures in Wonderland, Through the Looking Glass, and The Hunting of the Snark*, 1925.

Zondervan Publishing House: Lawrence O. Richards, *69 Ways to Start a Study Group and Keep It Growing*, 1973.

1

The Purpose of Small Groups

Jesus said unto him, Thou shalt love the Lord thy God with all thy heart, and with all thy soul, and with all thy mind. This is the first and great commandment. And the second is like unto it, Thou shalt love thy neighbour as thyself (Matt. 22:37-39).

Immediately, I understand that the God/man relationship is intended to be both vertical and horizontal. Too often, we focus on the vertical to the exclusion of the horizontal. And yet Jesus placed them on an equal basis. The first commandment is vertical; but He said, "The second *is like unto it,*" and it is horizontal. If there is a wide-open channel between my heart and God's, then that vertical flow will be so forceful that it must ever widen and lengthen the horizontal channel through which God flows *through me* to other men.

Draw
nigh
to
God,
and
he
will
draw
nigh
to
you. . . .
This is my commandment, That ye love one another, as I
have loved you (Jas. 4:8; John 15:12).

Over and over God expressed it.
If
ye
keep
my
commandments,
ye
shall
abide
in
my
love. . . .
These things I command you, that ye love one another
(John 15:10, 17).

This is God's command. Not that He thinks it would
be nice
        if we could work it into our schedules
        if we could place it in our activities
        if we could sing about it in church.
It is a fact that God's command is vertical/horizontal.

If we obey, we *will* keep the vertical relationship of

loving Him. If we obey, we *will* keep the horizontal relationship of loving those about us. All of those about us:

"Into all the world"
"Into the highways and hedges"
"With publicans and sinners"

The vertical demand is difficult: We are to bear the stamp of God. The horizontal demand, however, often jolts us like a live wire: We are *also* to display God in our lives to others. A Christian has been defined as a person whose life makes it easy for others to believe in God.

Vertical/Horizontal

God
loves
us
personally.
He
deals
with
us
uniquely.
Ours
is
a
One-to-one
relationship
on
the
vertical
plane.

But we are all His children; we are all to work together to build His kingdom; we are to love one another on the horizontal plane every day of our earthly lives.

The God/man relationship is vertical/horizontal.

17

As our vertical relationship bears the characteristics of Jesus, so will our horizontal relationship be intertwined with other people. And here is where many shrink inwardly. For it is often on the horizontal plane that the genuineness of our commitment on the vertical plane is most starkly spotlighted.

It is a rather simple thing to piously assert: "I love the Lord with all my heart, soul, mind, and strength." Self-delusion can easily be present vertically. Even hypocrisy. But it is more difficult to possess anything less than self-authenticity when, horizontally, one must reach out a hand of true love

> across the prejudices
> across the hatreds
> across the injustices
> across the hesitancies
> across the fears
> across the ugliness
> across the brutalities
> across the personality conflicts
> across the myriad spike-pointed barriers

that commonly separate people

from

people.

But when the vertical relationship is genuine, the horizontal relationship will be equally genuine. You can, then, look at the *loving God* and say:

You
are
my
Redeemer;
I
love
You.

and at the same moment
you can look at your
unloving neighbor and say:
You are my brother; you are my sister; I want to help you; I care about you.

The God/man relationship is vertical/horizontal.

It is on this foundation that we set the goal of the small-group structure within the church. In the regular program of an organization, it is often difficult for a person to get close to another. The larger the institution, the more limited people are in becoming personally interrelated. The quality of the minister/parishioner relationship in the sanctuary inspires vertical growth, but the impersonalization of our culture often denies horizontal growth even within the church.

In our society, we hide behind masks, sharing little of our inner heart with another. Many characterize the man in the street as one suffering from full-orbed loneliness. Too frequently, that same gnawing hunger for human companionship and caring is pervading the person sitting next to you in the church pew.

I believe this was a major concern of Jesus toward the close of His earthly ministry. In the last crucial hours before the Crucifixion (see John 13—17), He placed major emphasis on "the new commandment" which He so explicitly stated in John 15:12:

>*As*
>*I*
>*have*
>*loved*
>*you*
>*[so you] love one another.*

"As I have loved you."
How did Jesus love?

Completely. With self-abandonment
           With total involvement
           With full participation
           Selflessly

The depersonalization of our social system has struck deeply into the ministry of the church and stripped us of our ability to follow Jesus' "new commandment" to its fullest. For to love Jesus' way, we have to intimately know and deeply understand one another as persons. That dimension of love is possible only in settings of interpersonal involvement where honest, meaningful communication can occur.

And in our computerized culture, this may now be possible only in the small-group setting.

Even in the warmest, friendliest church, we don our nicest clothes, our most pleasing smiles, and our best cultivated manners. We respond to greetings that we are "fine," the weather is "beautiful," and the children are "all well." It is only in the eyes that the perceptive listener might see pain burning like twin martyr fires and understand the aching, strangling problems of our hearts.

But in our rushing society, even the perceptive cannot often linger to help. There are too many other pressures, too many other calls, too many other demands. So, with a sigh of relief, even the perceptive person scurries away, pretending to believe our lie that "all's right with the world."

The small-group concept can change all of that.

For the small-group concept means that, one night of the week, a group of persons clear their calendars of all social demands and pencil in their appointment with a few members of God's family. There an openness of heart can be engendered. In the homey, accepting atmosphere of one family's den, facades can be traded for reality.

20

Someone recently defined the old word *dialogue* as "the serious address and response of two or more persons in which the being and truth of each is confronted by the being and truth of the other." That kind of *dialogue* cannot occur in the large sanctuary with its structured service. It can take place only in the casual setting of the small group.

William Newell, in his book *Romans, Verse by Verse,* makes a significant statement:

> We must remember that in the early days of the Church, believers gathered in great simplicity, according to our Lord's Word, "where two or three are gathered together in My name, there am I in the midst of them" (Matt. 18:20). It is fast coming to this . . . [where people] are gathering more and more as the early Christians did—in homes, in Bible conferences, wherever Christ and His Word and real fellowship in the Spirit are the only drawing power.[1]

Especially note the elements Newell mentions and consider their possibilities in the small group.

1. Christ

Christ has promised to be present "where two or three are gathered together in my name" (Matt. 18:20). In a personally intimate way, Christ shares in this kind of encounter. He no longer is categorized as pulpit creed; He becomes vibrant, living Personality. He, the Redeemer from sin *and* circumstance, becomes central in the thinking, feeling, and decision-making of those "gathered" in His name. And in that setting, it becomes easier to accept His invitation: "Come unto me, all ye that labour and are heavy laden, and I will give you rest" (Matt. 11:28).

Gathered with a caring group of God-family members in a den or about a kitchen table, theological controversies and psychological hang-ups may fade away like mist in the morning sun as one understands that Jesus Christ himself *is* Christianity. He is alive *now*. He is actively, this minute, *involved* with each member of that small group. In a specially sacred way, Christ participates "where two or three are gathered together in [His] name."

2. His Word

Taken from the context of the authoritative minister-to-parishioner setting—or even the teacher-student arrangement in the church—God's Word can become intensely personal in heart-sharing. In the study of the Scriptures with a small group of friends, there is the possibility of saying: "Hey! Wait a minute! What does this *mean?* In very simple language, stop and tell me what this biblical injunction means to *me! now!*" And in such a setting, the Bible comes alive in areas hitherto misunderstood, unexplored, unexplained, undeveloped.

In the small-group context, truth is *shared* rather than *taught.* Through concrete life examples, one confronts the Christian demands of patience, trust, and faith. Through discussion, one begins to see that simple pat answers to life's dilemmas are not always available. Through guided biblical study, one can see that God does not function within a framework of trite cliches or vague formulas. Through God's Word, prayerfully considered with trusted friends, it is easier to see that God is *Love* dynamically making "all things work together for good to them that love God" (Rom. 8:28).

While the world talks about a generation gap, too many Christians suffer from a reality gap. Theological and practical inconsistencies cobweb the minds of many people. But in viable, earnest, nitty-gritty discussion within a small-group setting, the Bible can come alive

22

with a meaningful vitality and relevance never before known.

3. Real Fellowship in the Spirit

There is a difference between mere association and real "fellowship in the Spirit." Fellowship can be defined as a small group of persons doing things together like baseball, pizza feasts, and charades. Fellowship can be defined as a small group of persons talking about cars, football scores, or even Sunday School attendance. But real "fellowship in the Spirit" can be defined only in terms of a oneness, a unity, a *sharing* of the essential elements of human life.

In a small-group atmosphere, a common phrase may be: "I don't know why I'm telling you this, but somehow I think you might understand." This sense of acceptance, coupled with the release of spirit-sharing, is a vital characteristic of a real "fellowship in the Spirit." For we all so desperately *need* the horizontal relationship with each other.

Many times, the touch of a human hand can stimulate tears to wipe a messy situation clean.

Many times, the love in a human voice can be the catalyst for an outpouring of one's total spirit to God.

Many times, the concern of a human heart can modify, even erase, deep-rooted fears.

Many times, the concerted *caring* of a human group can melt rigid hate molds and make ready God's remolding of an entire life.

The writer to the Hebrews said: "Let us think of one another and how we can encourage one another to love and do good deeds. . . . Let us do all we can to help one another's faith" (Heb. 10:24-25, Phillips).

We need each other. God has given us each other.

23

But we have to draw *near* to each other in the fellowship of His Spirit in small, interpersonal contexts. We grow vertically in the church sanctuary; we grow horizontally in holding human hands.

In our depersonalized society, the church, too frequently, is missing the New Testament level of Christian brotherhood which caused people in the first century to remark: "Behold! How they love one another!" In our whirling, pressurized culture people are longing for dialogue, not monologue. People who commune vertically still have deep need to touch humanly.

In the small-group context, the vertical/horizontal of the God/man relationship may and should be enhanced. True love can then flow in both directions.

2

The Structure of Small Groups

A lion used to prowl about a field in which four oxen used to dwell. Many a time, he tried to attack them; but whenever he came near, they turned their tails to one another, so that whichever way he approached them, he was met by the horns of one of them. At last, however, they fell a-quarrelling among themselves, and each went off to pasture alone in a separate corner of the field. Then the lion attacked them one by one and soon made an end to all four.

—*Aesop's Fables* (ca. 600 B.C.)

The fable illustrates Aristotle's dictum that the object of every association is some good. When the oxen formed a "small group," they performed the *function* of warding off danger. Because they were *interdependent*, they found their contact *meaningful* and *reward-*

25

ing. With their own unique system of *communicating*, they formed an *interaction system* which exerted *co-equal effects* upon the identity of the system. Aristotle was correct in this instance: The association of the four oxen was for good.

We have already discussed the concept of *people* in small groups. It seems that the distinguishing factor between a small group and a collection of people is its *purpose*. And, as the fable illustrates, when a small group forms *on purpose*, its purpose is "some good."

The unique purpose of small groups within the church structure is the opportunity for development of the horizontal/vertical God/man relationship.

> As
> I
> have
> loved
> you
> [So you] love one another (John 15:12).

Since that is a praiseworthy purpose, it illustrates Aristotle's dictum that the object of every association is some good.

In the simple fable are some elements that may easily be seen in the small-group context. These were derived from scholars who have attempted to define the phenomenon.

A small group has been defined as:

1. "A collection of individuals whose existence as a collection is *rewarding* to the individuals."[1]

2. "Two or more persons who come into contact for a purpose and who consider the *contact meaningful*."[2]

3. "An organized system of two or more individuals who are interrelated so that the system *performs an important function*."[3]

26

4. "A collection of individuals who have relations to one another that make them *interdependent* to some significant degree."[4]

5. "A number of persons who *communicate* with one another often enough over a span of time, and who are few enough so that each person is able to communicate with all the others, not at secondhand, through other people, but *face to face*."[5]

6. "*An open interaction system* in which actions determine the structure of the system and successive interactions *exert coequal effects upon the identity of the system*."[6]

Meshing these scholastic views, we find that the small group is valuable. Because people are by nature *interdependent*, they find the caring friendship of a small group *rewarding* and the human contact *meaningful*. Their study of the Word of God and sharing life experiences *performs an important function* for them. In an impersonal society, they have the human yearning for *face-to-face communication* with other humans fulfilled. Together, they form *an interaction system which exerts coequal effects upon the identity of the system.*

Aristotle's dictum may be found to be as valid for people as for oxen. The association formed in a small group is for "good."

Bypassing an attempt to define a small group, John K. Brilhart listed its major characteristics as follows:

1. A number of people sufficiently small for each to be aware of and have some reaction to each other (from 2 to rarely more than 20).

2. A mutually interdependent purpose in which the success of each is contingent upon the success of the others in achieving this goal.

3. Each person has a sense of belonging or member-

ship, identifying himself with the other members of the groups.

4. Oral interaction (not all of the interaction will be oral, but a significant characteristic of the small group is reciprocal influence exercised by talking).

5. Behavior based on norms and procedures accepted by all members.[7]

How Many?

Brilhart mentions that the group should be "sufficiently small" for personal awareness and reaction. In further discussion of this, he says:

> The number of persons forming a group is a major determinant of what happens during discussions. A person needs to be flexible in adjusting to groups of different size. As group size increases, the complexity increases rapidly; the number of interpersonal relationships increases geometrically as the number of members increases arithmetically. Thus a group of two people has one interpersonal relationship; a group of three people has three; a group of five people has ten; a group of ten people has forty-five; a group of twenty people has 190 relationships.
>
> Increased size means less opportunity for the average participant to speak and to influence others. ... Frustration increases with group size. In larger groups, the less forceful and confident discussants speak less, while the more forceful tend to occupy an even greater proportion of the time. There is a tendency for one central person to do a proportionately greater amount of talking. Also speeches tend to be longer, often including several points not particularly pertinent to the issue of the moment.[8]

As group size increases, more centralized control of procedures is needed. The atmosphere becomes more formal. There is less hope of heart-sharing. The larger the group size, the more tightly the masks are glued on.

Brilhart states further:

Other effects commonly occurring when group size increases include greater difficulty in establishing criteria or values, more time reaching a decision, lowering of cohesiveness (attractiveness to the group), and a tendency for cliques to develop within the group.

How large should a discussion group be? . . . If the purpose is to encourage individual questioning and thinking, choose a small group.[9]

Since 10 people involve 45 interpersonal relationships, this would seem a substantial number for a good starter size. For our purposes within the church, the group should probably rarely exceed 15 in number.

Where Is the Small Group?

The small group will probably meet in the same home at the same time on the same night/day of the week. The host and hostess should strive to make the atmosphere as relaxed and informal as possible. It may be that refreshments will be helpful in "breaking the ice" and keeping things moving. If refreshments are served, keep them simple and easily within reach of self-service. A hostess constantly moving to fill coffee cups or pass around trays of cupcakes will detract from the whole point of the evening. So if you use refreshments, be certain they work *for* the group goal; *keep them unobtrusive.*

Where Are the Children?

Baby-sitting is often a necessity. If that is true for your group, acquire a group sitter and share the costs. If possible, have the children in a different home from the small-group meeting to avoid distraction. If this is not feasible, do arrange for them to be in the most distant part of the house.

How Long Is a Small Group?

The small-group meeting should probably be designed to fill an hour and a half. The goal could be to spend 30 minutes with the structured Bible study text or discipling curriculum, the next 30 minutes spent in free discussion. The final 30 minutes may be spent in fellowship.

Make it a firm rule to begin and conclude on time. This should be something on which members can depend in the planning of their schedules. No matter how interested everyone is at the designated time for closing, promptness is important because of other responsibilities and commitments.

Because of the importance of strict timekeeping, strive to limit socializing at the beginning to a minimum. When it is time to begin, introduce new people, welcome everyone, bow for an opening prayer, *and begin.* An hour of important work is at hand. Don't waste a minute of it.

Where Does the Small Group Fit?

As we have discussed, the *purpose* of the small group is *ministry.* Its structure is to provide opportunity for development of the vertical/horizontal, God/man relationship with a few trusted friends. It is an invaluable tool in Kingdom building.

It must, however, be kept in mind that it is not an entity within itself. It is a part of the larger Body, the Church. Although the small group should never become simply a means for Sunday School recruitment, church attendance should constantly be encouraged. There should be no pressure to join the local Nazarene church, for the universal Church is our concern; however, the command of God for the meetings and sacraments of His Church as an entire family should be stressed.

There will, of course, be the tendency for most members to gravitate toward the local Nazarene church because that is where their friends in the small group, for the most part, attend. Be sure those who are unchurched are *invited* and feel that a welcome awaits them at the church if and when they choose to come. Make plans to take these "outreach" persons involved in your small group with you or other group members to church services and, later, for lunch or coffee. Pique their interest in attendance at special occasions in the church community. Introduce them to other people of the church. Arrange social events where they can widen their acquaintances within the congregation. Do all within your power to make the unchurched in your small group feel just as *accepted* and *wanted* within the body of the church as they do in your home.

Another important service you should offer unchurched members is to introduce the pastor of your church as the spiritual leader on whom you rely. From his ministry, you should quote him as the dominant, respected authority. Arrange times when he can meet personally with your small group. If you have a video-cassette machine available, you might even ask him to do a series of sermonettes from which your small-group discussion could springboard for the evening.

Those who are not active in a church structure should be inspired to trust him in the pastoral capacity whenever they have need. If they attend a service with you, be sure he meets them personally. If they need a special touch, schedule a time for a brief get-acquainted conference. If they have life-shattering problems, suggest his God-anointed counselling.

In our culture, where the fashion is to believe in no absolutes, trust in no one's integrity, and yield to no authority, the *need* for a pastor is, perhaps, the greatest

31

in human history. Although adults, we know we are not wise enough to guide our lives. We need the security of a man of God who can point us to the *absolutes* with personal integrity and divine authority. You can give this gift to the members of your small group by presenting your pastor to them at his best.

Who, Then, Composes a Small Group?

That is your choice. It could begin with you and your neighbors. You might be the only "churched" person in the group. You would initiate such a small group by chatting with your neighbors about their interest in Bible study. If they manifest a desire, then begin formally planning to make it a weekly "happening" in your home.

It could begin with a few people from the church who each bring friends. This larger nucleus of churched people may strengthen the discussions, but that is not necessarily true. Much is dependent upon each situation's unique characteristics. God will have to lead you in the best approach for you.

Of course a small group, as we discuss it here, could be composed of totally churched people who feel the need for Christian companionship and sharing. But that is often best supplied through Sunday School classes, personal friends, etc. The major thrust of what we are discussing now about the small-group context inside the church structure is one that is bent on *ministry* both to the churched and to the unchurched who will come to your house for coffee and Bible study, but who would not likely agree to go to church with you!

Since this is the major goal, as presented in this book, the small group is an ever-evolving, ever-changing, ever-developing phenomenon. As the number of group members grow, the "cell" will need to be divided to keep it sufficiently small. When new people become interested in the study, an additional group may need to be formed to let them begin at the beginning of the course in which you may now be in the middle. For these reasons, the constitution of the small group is constantly dynamic.

Training the Small-Group Leader

Because of this dynamism, the group leader will be training another group leader from the first meeting. When choosing an assistant who will, ultimately, head up a small group of his own, look for a person who will pray with you for the group on a regular basis. At that weekly meeting, discuss with him/her the events of the previous sessions and how its effectiveness could have been improved. His/her observations will make you a better leader because he/she is not under the pressure of leading the small group at the time. So be open to learn from your trainee.

Ask your potential group leader to observe the leadership skills you have learned and are attempting to practice. Discuss their reasons, strengths, and weaknesses. Encourage constant observation of these elements in action within the small group. This training time spent with your assistant can be as valuable to you as to him/her. Weekly discussion of the interactions and needs of guiding a group of people can be vital.

When the time comes for him/her to take the role of small-group leader, be available to give advice and encouragement. Your tasks in God's kingdom building are of inestimable worth.

3

The Leadership of Small Groups

Like the happy centipede, many people get along fine working with others without thinking about which foot to put forward. But when one is assigned the responsibility of *leading* a group of "others," there is the call to study. It is a demanding role that does not come easily.

Irving Lee wrote an insightful little book, *How to Talk with People.* In it, he discussed the "tired leader" who "begrudged the amount of effort it took to get people to talk and think together."[1] The person asked to be a small-group leader must examine his own motives, his own approach to the problem and persons involved, and his own capacities for selflessness, to decide whether he is willing to expend the time and energy required for leadership. George Homans has stressed the need for the leader to know himself as follows:

He may be the most active member of the group, and yet he must often keep silent. He must live up most fully to the group norms, and yet he, more than anyone else, must resolve conflicts of norms. More than anyone else, he has the ends of the group at heart.[2]

Leadership is a vital, even awesome, task.

Tannenbaum, Weschler, and Massarik have defined leadership as "interpersonal influence, exercised in given situations and directed, through the communication process, toward the attainment of a specified goal or goals."[3] Having made this general definition, let us discuss the major components: (1) Interpersonal influence; (2) The situation; (3) The communication process; and (4) The goal.

1. Interpersonal Influence

The essence of leadership is interpersonal influence, involving the guide in an attempt to affect the decisions of the discussants through communication. Sol Levine has listed four kinds of leaders:

1. The Charismatic Leader who affects and inspires his membership by the strong expression of his emotionality
2. The Organizational Leader who drives members to action
3. The Intellectual Leader who is able to provide perspective but is unfortunately often quite inadequate at the "working out" stage
4. The Informal Leader who possesses an acute sensitivity to the feelings of the members and his ability to work with people in a warm, flexible way[4]

Although there will probably be personality traits of each of these leader-types present, the one most effective in the small-group situation within the church is the last. The informal leader is a departure from the general cultural conception of a Superman who has all wisdom and possesses all skill. R. M. Stogdill listed the accepted societal characteristics of a good leader as a person with:

1. Capacity (intelligence, alertness, verbal facility, originality, judgment)
2. Achievement (scholarship, knowledge, athletic accomplishment)
3. Responsibility (dependability, initiative, persistence, aggressiveness, self-confidence, desire to excel)
4. Participation (activity, sociability, cooperation, adaptability, humor)
5. Status (socioeconomic position, popularity)[5]

Although such an overachiever might exist in Utopia, this is not the profile of the person needed to lead in a small-group situation whose purpose is *ministry*. In the light of the needs of the church ministry of small groups, the term has been redefined in terms of the following basic tenets:

1. Small-group leaders are regular people, not one-man dynamos who know all the answers and do all the work.
2. Small-group leaders are developed; they are not born with a mysterious charismatic ability; they study rules, techniques, interaction problems, and *grow.*
3. Small-group leaders like to work with and are sensitive to other people.
4. Small-group leaders don't need to keep up a front of always being poised, independent, and decisive.[6]

We defined *leadership* as "interpersonal influence" which is the acceptance of the "informal leader" role. This consists principally of responding to, understanding, and guiding other people's feelings. He is able to exert interpersonal influence without giving up any of his warm, informal characteristics. He is a leading member

36

of the group, but shows no inclination to emphasize dominance and power. The interpersonal influence is sensitive, open, and flexible.

2. The Situation

The concept *situation* denotes any elements in the social or cultural context that affect the interaction of leader and group. Some of these would be:

a. Physical phenomena (noise, light, table and chair arrangement, etc.)

b. Other individuals, including the members of the specific group of which the leader and members are a part

c. The organization

d. The broader culture, including social norms, role prescriptions, stereotypes, etc.

e. Goals, including personal goals, group goals, and organizational goals[7]

Each small group meeting on the same night with the same goals and the same number will be different, not only because of the personalities involved, but because of the situation of the group. The leader must be aware of the influence of these elements.

a. The chosen placing of physical facilities in close proximity so that people can be near each other is a vital influence on successful interaction. Consider the "small" item of good ventilation. Note the leader's need for alertness in this diagrammed situation:

Place→	Group	Leader→	Place→	Group
(Stuffy)	members→	(Reacts	(Opens	members
	(Drowsy)	to	windows)	(More alert)
		lethargy)		

b. The inclusion of members other than those usually in the group will affect the situation. Responding to all group members and working for the most open, honest interaction is vital. Remember that each person in the group has social values, economic values, political values, educational values, aesthetic values, as well as spiritual and moral values. The blending of this polyglot of individuals forms a situation unique in all the world. The leader must be aware and work within it.

c. The organizational flow of the activities is a part of the situation. Time is an important element here, for the leader is schedule-bound and must adjust to the time allotted for the discussion. Impatience is a general characteristic among busy people, and a leader who willfully disregards time creates a serious strain on the situation. Listener moods, attitudes, feelings, and desires which are affected by the hour of the day, the day of the week, and the season of the year, must also be considered. The buoyant mood of a couple just returned from their honeymoon will definitely be a factor in the small-group situation. The fact that you set up the Christmas tree and your den is decked with holly for a specific meeting will also affect the situation in which your group studies. Shocking news events of a big fire or race riot will be in the minds of your group. The most successful leader will understand these factors and organize the flow of activities to build upon them rather than attempting to override or ignore.

d. You, as a group leader, can pretty well determine the effect of the broader culture on the situation of your small group. In order to establish some uniformity and avoid embarrassment, you may want to make some facts known to the group members prior to the first meeting. This might include such things as:

- Come in casual dress.
- Plan to sit on blankets in the backyard (if it is an outdoor setting).

- No scholarly commentaries allowed.
- The leader is not addressed as "Sir" or "Madam" or by any formal title.

Good advice is: "When in Rome, do as the Romans do." It may be helpful for any first-comers to know "what the Romans do" in relation to the broader culture of American social norms, role prescriptions, stereotypes, etc.

e. Within the situation is also the powerful influence of goals. The leader should be cognizant of the compelling personal goals of each group member such as self-importance, self-preservation, development of a satisfying life philosophy, satisfaction of innate curiosity, and, certainly, the satisfactions of companionship and mutual fulfillment of each other's mental, social, and spiritual needs.

Also affecting the situation are the group goals of Bible understanding and applying truths. Comprehending and applying these precepts to a hectic, demanding, often frustrating life is the goal for participants. But differences of opinion can create tensions that the leader must deal with in the situation itself. Certainly controversy arising out of the fulfillment of these goals influences the situation of the entire group.

A group leader in one of my pastorates says that his most spirit-cringing memory is a near-melee that developed when a woman was wrestling with the command: "Be still, and know that I am God" (Ps. 46:10). A divorcee, she worked 40 hours a week as a registered nurse where there was constant pressure. When she returned each day to her 14-room house, she faced the problem of keeping it clean, the half-acre yard mowed, the garden tilled, the vegetables canned, and her three small children cared for. She said, in tears, "When I get still, I go to sleep!"

Another group member, a lady who did not work outside the home and had only one child who was in college, took instant issue that the lady's problem was a spiritual one. If she truly loved God, she would find a way to stay alertly awake in His presence for the hours that the housewife demanded of herself.

As group leader, you are working in the situation where people's demands, comprehension levels, frames of reference, etc., are diverse. Ever be alert that "leadership is interpersonal influence [which you have probably always understood] *exercised in given situations* [which you may have overlooked, but which is of vital concern]."

3. The Communication Process

Communication means, literally, to "make common"—that is, to create in a receiver's mind an idea or image similar to the one in the mind of the sender. That is not as simple as it sounds. Meaning must be transmitted, not transferred. The sender translates his thought or image into language symbols in a code familiar to both parties; then he must transmit these symbols and hope they will be intercepted and received by the listener. In between there are many opportunities for problems to develop.

The model on the following page suggests some of the possibilities for mishap as the message is transferred from the source to the receiver.

Each person in the small group speaks from his unique level of communication expertise; from his attitudes biased and molded on personal life experiences; from his knowledge gained from a family, socioeconomic, academic background peculiar to himself; from a social system that has its own sets of roles, values, understandings, even language; and from a culture that may be as diverse from the culture of another group member as

40

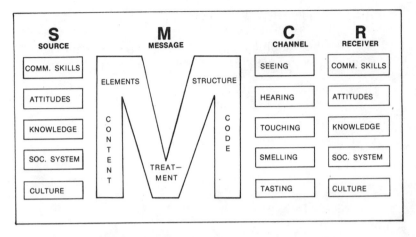

S SOURCE	M MESSAGE	C CHANNEL	R RECEIVER
COMM. SKILLS	ELEMENTS / STRUCTURE	SEEING	COMM. SKILLS
ATTITUDES		HEARING	ATTITUDES
KNOWLEDGE	C O N T E N T / C O D E	TOUCHING	KNOWLEDGE
SOC. SYSTEM	TREAT—MENT	SMELLING	SOC. SYSTEM
CULTURE		TASTING	CULTURE

A model of the ingredients in communication.[8]

the two poles. It is possible that Archie Bunker and Michael Stivik could be in your small group at the same time. That TV show can give you insight into the problems involved in communication as illustrated by Berlo's model.

The speaker (or source) has an idea he wants to communicate; he filters it through all the items mentioned above; he chooses its coded, treated content. It is then "sent" through the channels of the five senses to be "received" by the "listeners," each of whom filters that chosen coded content through: his own communication expertise; his own attitudes biased and molded on personal life experiences; his own knowledge gained from a family, socioeconomic, academic background peculiar to himself; his own social system that has its own sets of roles, values, understandings, even language; and his own culture that may be as diverse from the speaker's as the two poles.

41

Communication is complex. The miracle is that it occurs as often as it does!

Another helpful diagram is this one by Jane Blankenship. It gives an overview of the communicative event.

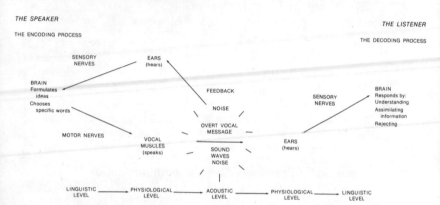

THE SPEAKER

THE ENCODING PROCESS

THE LISTENER

THE DECODING PROCESS

SENSORY NERVES

EARS (hears)

BRAIN Formulates ideas Chooses specific words

FEEDBACK

NOISE

SENSORY NERVES

BRAIN Responds by: Understanding Assimilating information Rejecting

MOTOR NERVES

VOCAL MUSCLES (speaks)

OVERT VOCAL MESSAGE

SOUND WAVES NOISE

EARS (hears)

LINGUISTIC LEVEL ———→ PHYSIOLOGICAL LEVEL ———→ ACOUSTIC LEVEL ———→ PHYSIOLOGICAL LEVEL ———→ LINGUISTIC LEVEL

An overview of the communicative event[9]

I find this overview helpful in that it identifies the communication process from the idea in the brain of the speaker through all of the various filters to the brain of the listener. It also identifies the various levels that are constantly affecting the success or failure of the efforts to share.

Before a word is spoken, the idea is filtered through all the elements specified in Berlo's model into specific utterances (linguistic level) through his individual physiological level which passes through the acoustic level, with all its noises that might be present (e.g., children playing, airplane flying overhead, sprinkler on the lawn) through the physiological level of the listener who accepts it through his filters (as described by Berlo) into his brain.

42

Some portions of his response will serve as feedback cues for the source, who can then try to adjust or restate if he perceives that he has been/is being misunderstood. Other portions of the listener's response may be verbal, so then the listener becomes a speaker "sending" a brain idea, and the former speaker becomes the listener receiving and providing feedback.

The good leader of a small group must be ever cognizant of the difficulties inherent in the communication process and be constantly striving to understand each member's feedback so that, in the circular response of speaker and listener changing and adapting roles, the leader can help rectify confusion, dissolve anger, or heal wounded feelings.

Again, "Leadership is interpersonal influence, exercised in given situations and directed, through the communication process, toward the attainment of a specified goal or goals."

4. The Goal

All group leadership acts are focused toward a goal. To the leader of a small group, the group is a reality because of specific purposes. Because of the importance of those purposes, in the church structure, he believes that he is responsible for directing the group to personal fulfillments. He works on the foundation of a creed in which faith in the individual's ability to work within the group and trust in the integrity of group decisions is basic. Therefore, he has respect for the ability of the group involving self-direction at times, critical thinking in points of study, resistance to unacceptable or defenseless influences, and appropriate problem-solving behavior.

There will always be elements both negative and positive germinating in each group in the work toward goals. The leader must understand that this is a part of any human group because participants come from diverse backgrounds, diverse perception levels, diverse current problems. The leader himself must accept each person's unique worth and strive to impress that upon every group member.

A pointed poem that goes to the root of this understanding is one my wife often quotes, though she does not know its source.

> If I could only know the road you came,
> The jagged rocks or crooked ways,
> I would more kindly think of your missteps
> And only praise.
>
> If I could know the heartaches you have felt,
> The longings for the things that never came;
> I would more kindly judge your erring then
> Nor even blame.

When a group leader has that kind of heart empathy with each member, he is able to have deep respect for his efforts even though they may crude, rude, or abrasive. With the heart empathy of the poem, he can attempt to see each person in God's family as having particular worth and significance which is totally unrelated to social class, occupational status, personal traits, skills, abilities, appearance, race, or other such characteristics. The significance of each individual lies in his/her being a beloved child of God, created in the Father's image. Only when the small-group leader can truly perceive each member in this way, no matter how unlovely he may appear on the surface, can the leader be at his best in seeking the fulfillment of the purposes of the small group within the dynamics of the church.

Obviously, he cannot begin to measure up to this

theoretical demand unless he has a vital and close relationship with Christ himself. When the leader can be Christ-dominated and -controlled, there is the opportunity for all purposes of the small group to find fruition. Without this personal relationship, the leader is without message and spends his time attempting to moralize or deal in clichés. Unless he is experientially rooted and grounded in biblical truths himself, he cannot *minister* dynamically within the small-group cell.

4

Characteristics of Leaders

Some characteristics of successful small-group leaders are listed here as compiled from the writings of such experts in communication as Halbert Gulley, George Homans, George Brilhart, and others.

1. The leader should be fully indoctrinated in the purpose for each specific meeting.

2. The leader should, in that light, organize carefully the approach to be taken, the problems to be met, and the steps toward achieving the meeting goal.

3. The leader should have as many stimulating questions listed with his notes as possible. His goal is interaction, not lecture.

4. The leader should attempt to enhance the prestige of each member in the meeting. Even though a member may sincerely believe in the value of the group, if he feels that his personal worth to the group is slight,

he lacks, in Durkheim's words, *solidaire* with the group. The leader should be on the alert to find ways to increase feelings of individual merit.[1]

5. The leader should stress the importance of the unity of these individuals, thus increasing feelings of cohesiveness. "We are working together on this in love" is a tremendous emotional gift to human hearts who so often feel their struggle is solitary.

6. The leader will attempt to help members accept group purposes and remain in line with those purposes in discussion. It is very easy to get sidetracked in all kinds of fascinating bypaths. The leader must ask his group to work with him in staying on the "main road" that leads to the specific attainment of the group purpose.

7. The leader should attempt to bring all members into the discussion and avoid divisiveness. Including members can be done by direct questions (e.g., "John, what do you think?") or by overhead questions to the group but looking directly at John so that he knows the leader is inviting his response.

8. The leader should encourage reflective thought. He should strive to build an atmosphere where members can enjoy inquiry in discussion. There should be an aura of excitement in searching for God-knowledge, God-perceptions, and God-solutions to human problems. A group that has the feeling of absorption in the adventure of investigation will be more cohesive than any other.

9. The leader must be open-minded. He will listen without fear of threat, suspend judgment, and encourage full consideration of minority points of view. Norman Maier describes a "Risk Technique" for allowing members to voice opinions that are not normally the accepted ones. He suggests that the leader set aside a special peri-

od in the discussion during which members are asked to talk about the *risks* of accepting a particular position, belief, or tenet. In this period, Maier feels that members are less nervous about expressing doubts, reservations, even hostilities to what is being generally accepted by the group. "The risk technique was developed," he said, "to aid the emotionally involved discussion leader in listening, accepting, and understanding."[2] It also has the added benefit of stimulating interaction for all participants in a situation that might seem threatening to some.

10. The leader has respect for and a sensitivity toward others. He acts with tact and concern for each member's feelings. He reacts to statements with acceptance, even when he may disagree personally. He merely asks to know how they think and why. One of my professors at the University of Kansas used to come around his desk to study the person with "different" ideas and say: "Tell me more." I thought it was an excellent way to allow the member to maintain respect and have further opportunity for presenting his case. Sometimes, in the explanation, most of the group would agree; if not, he still was given the full respect of "Tell me more about your idea; I value it because it came from you. Whether or not I agree is of no consequence in my respect for you."

11. The leader will try to refrain from speaking in the language of argumentation. He is careful never to attack a person when disagreeing, but to focus closely on issues rather than the wisdom of the contributor.

12. The leader will keep an antenna attuned to the emotional climate of the group, noting when members are unhappy, when they are on the verge of consensus, or when a hesitant member wants to speak. He never takes sides in a personal conflict.

13. The leader is a good listener. In many ways, his main function is to be involved in *listening* so he can understand and clarify for the rest of the group that which may be unclear. He is careful about interrupting speakers unless a dominating member is talking too much of the time.

14. The leader is always attempting to summarize accurately what has been said, as he understands it. One question that should often recur is: "Are we agreed, then, that we want to define this term in this way?" or whatever problem the group is wrestling with. He is constantly summarizing, restating, and stressing agreement.

15. The leader speaks well. His remarks should be well planned in advance; his organization of discussion leading should be precise; his points that he wants to bring out should be pertinent. This takes work, but it is essential.

16. The leader is flexible. Although the leader has an organization on paper or in mind as to how he will guide the discussion, he is sensitive to what is happening in the group in that situation at that time. With that sensitivity, he will adjust his behavior and plans to do whatever is needed to help the group *where they are at that time in that place* toward the group goal. It may completely bypass everything he has meticulously planned. So be it. The *needs* of the group are more important than outline-following!

17. The leader is calm and self-controlled. If he loses his "cool," the group will invariably be harmed. An excellent model of this characteristic is the courtroom judge who must maintain his perspective and thoughtful patience at all times.

18. The leader is never afraid to say, "I don't know." His function is not to be Superknowledge. He is a guide.

If he honestly does not know the answer to a complexity, there are probably many other great minds who do not know it either! There is no merit in being a know-it-all. If the leader feels he must always have a ready answer, his group leadership will turn into a lecture where free-wheeling questions are not comfortable because they could push him into a realm where he is not expert . . . and the whole purpose of the small group would be lost.

19. The leader shares rewards of the search in his summaries and gives credit to the group. He readily praises the group for successes, always stressing the joint-ness of efforts.

20. The leader affirms confidence in the group. He underlines their findings, and when they are stumped, he asks something like: "Why don't we take a moment and think carefully? I know you can answer this. You always do." This inspires the members and stimulates response from all.

21. The leader is not afraid of silence. Our culture has inbred in most of us almost a terror when things get still. If we are alone, we race to the radio, stereo, or TV to break the silence. If we are with someone, we burst out in rashes of nervous chatter. The group who is truly thinking and working on heart-problems will need si-lence, many times, to do their best. Long periods, of course, are not necessary. But when natural silences come, accept them and be comfortable.

22. The leader gets excited over the discoveries of group members. Although it may be "old hat" to the leader, it is still glorious to that person who may have glimpsed a life-changing truth for the first time. The leader dare not squelch that enthusiasm with a superior attitude; rather, he should get excited with him and show it!

23. The leader has a sense of humor. Many times people can become so intense in hammering out ideas, humor may be truly needed to reduce tension. Lee wrote:

> When men are driven, they lose spontaneity and the zestful interest in what goes on. . . . There is a very real danger that our concern with improving human communication may lead members to forget the human part of the matter. . . . We need efficiency *and* satisfyingness. One may try to rig a discussion in the image of a belt line; if he succeeds he may find that those who attend become as inert as machines without the capacity (or will) to create.

> [To maintain a balance in discussion] listen with lessened tension when the bent to comedy or diversion or personal release is being manifested . . . [and] pick up the problem *after* the camaraderie or tension has been spent.[3]

24. The leader uses relevant illustrations, even visualizations. He should develop a file that will be a resource channel for him in his weekly preparations. Eye-catchers and ear-catchers capture human interest. A cartoon, a story, a newspaper headline, a picture, a personal anecdote—any simple illustration will communicate more readily than the complex. He encourages group members also to bring illustrations and visualizations that may help in meeting the goals of the group.

25. The leader is objective in receiving ideas. He understands that all knowledge and perception is subject to the idiosyncracies of the human observers. No one knows everything about anything, so he strives to keep a mood of open-minded inquiry, always implying, "Tell me more!" to encourage a yet greater response from all group members.

26. The leader is constantly seeking to prevent any member from losing face in the give-and-take of discus-

sion. When this happens, it can cause a serious problem. The member may withdraw, become aggressive, or go away. Cooperation between people in a small group must be based on mutual respect, goodwill, and all, especially the leader, working to give each member a feeling of special worth.

27. The leader accepts himself. Shakespeare wrote: "To thine own self be true, / And it must follow, as the night the day, / Thou canst not then be false to any man." Before he can accept and respect others, he must first accept and respect himself. Jesus said: "Thou shalt love thy neighbour as thyself" (Matt. 19:19). If he has doubts about self-competency, he should prepare thoroughly for each meeting. This will take away much of the butterfly stomp in the stomach and will keep him from falling into the trap of being either arrogant or self-denigrating. He should observe others' reactions and listen to himself. The leader must have objectivity for all group members; that includes himself.

28. The leader truly desires to communicate with each member. He is careful to keep eye contact consistent at all times with the group; never just the members of the group who are leaning his way. Speaking to only a few, with eye contact, restricts spontaneity and participation of the entire group.

29. The leader is always attempting to relate contributions, developing and supporting each to a solution that is acceptable to the group. One assist in this is to keep answering three basic questions: (a) What is the point? (b) How do you know? (c) How does it matter at this time?

30. The leader maintains perspective: perspective on the expenditure of time; perspective on new ideas (remembering that every new idea in the world was, at its

birth, in a minority of one!); perspective when pet ideas have been rejected.

31. The leader sets a tone so that members, including himself, always understand that when a suggested idea is squashed by the group, it is only the rejection of an *idea*. It has nothing whatever to do with rejection or denigration of the person who offered the idea. This cannot be overstressed.

32. The leader is enthusiastic. The reason the leader is willing to spend his time, efforts, and energies in the small-group preparation and discussion is because he wants to *minister* for God in this close interpersonal way. But the excitement for the joy of learning more of the God/man relationship is basically generated by the group leader. In a group where there are many unchurched, enthusiasm should especially be a dominant keynote.

33. The leader makes applications to the group. The leader spends enough time with God prior to the group discussion that God can speak through His Word in such a way that people can comprehend how those principles actually *do* apply in daily life. The Holy Spirit will highlight passages if there is an openness to such leading. He learns applications from study and from his own life, and is willing to share.

34. The leader prepares application questions. Examples are: "What does this mean to you?" "Is there anything you can do in the light of this *now?*" Openness on the part of the leader will stimulate equal openness by the group in finding and sharing applications.

35. The leader strives for restraint. In effective group guidance, the value of restraint in the use of power is evidenced by the leader's display of emotional balance in his relationship with each group member. The leader

has a large visibility in the group and, therefore, his actions will be interpreted in some sense as granting "goodness" or "badness" labels to actions of members. Restraint leads to fairness and gives security to the group. They receive neither outlandish praise or the brunt of hostile criticism.

36. The leader is predictable. Impulsiveness and instability give a group situation an aura of uncertainty which will lessen members' interest in coming. Even if the leader's personal nature is impulsive, he should work to hold it in check.

37. The leader does not monopolize. He understands that he is a guide; he is not a lecturer.

5

The Functions of Leaders

Group leaders have some basic responsibilities that are universally accepted: notifying members of meetings having all physical facilities ready, trying to make the climate (physiological and emotional) secure, etc. Let us consider some additional leadership functions.

1. The leader guides the discussion. He gets the group started; he announces the topic; he distributes material needed in the study; he announces any rules of procedure that might not be known to all; he suggests an outline for group thinking on the particular problem under consideration in this session; he asks the group to accept or modify it as a map-plan, etc.

2. The leader makes notes of progress. This can be done on a pad in his hand to which he frequently refers. It is best done on a chalkboard where all can see it. This alleviates the tendency to digress from the specific focal

point of the discussion. This also assists in making clear transitions from step to step. This also aids the leader's summarizing of what he feels has been accomplished so that he may ask the question: "Then is it true that we all agree . . .?" and be able to move on to another point. This also helps verify that the major topics or phrases are thoroughly discussed.

3. The leader encourages the reticent members to speak. He never embarrasses; but through his eye contact and occasional questions like "Joe, do you want to react to that idea?" he lets the shy member know he wants his participation and values his ideas.

4. The leader restrains the compulsive speakers who want to give long speeches or who want to speak so often that they dominate. Specific guidance on how to handle this difficulty is given in the chapter on leadership problems.

5. The leader rebounds questions to the group. Unless the leader is the only person qualified to answer on some point, he should always refer questions to other members. His function is to *guide*. Whenever anyone else present can deal with a subject, he should encourage him to do so. If a member asks for the leader's opinion, he might reply: "Well, let's see how other group members feel about this."

6. The leader speaks only when necessary. He does not feel compelled to comment after each member has spoken. He is a guide.

7. The leader reacts with acceptance and without evaluation. He may ask for clarification or elaboration of a comment. He may suggest additional explanation of stated views. He does not evaluate those views *ever* as good or bad! If evaluation seems necessary at some

point, he invites it from other members with questions such as "How well does that agree with other information we have?"

8. The leader does not panic when ideas are articulated that are obviously out of line with the Christian viewpoint. Comments that can aid a leader in maintaining calm (and not making the member who offered the comment feel he has been condemned) are: "That's an interesting observation," and go on with other discussion. Or he might ask: "What does someone else think?" If members might tend to be harsh in response, it might be better to ask someone to read scriptures that would be applicable and would lead the discussion into the Christian concept smoothly. Mistakes are part of the price of learning. This is why unchurched people may be found in a small group. They may not know even the basics of the Christian life. The leader is careful not to build barriers when they express views incompatible with Christ's teachings. They don't *know* yet, but that is the entire purpose of your being together. But the *learning* part of it must be without making the learnee feel stupid or condemned.

9. The leader's function is to guide dialogue; he is rarely in a position where he must deliver a monologue.

10. The leader reacts silently. Although he should avoid verbal "That's good" or "That's bad" comments, it is important for him to nod to all contributors to indicate their words have been heard and understood and their comments respected. Thus the leader is participating, but only in the supportive, silent role. Especially when an infrequent participant speaks, the leader should be sure that his eyes are warmly responsive. A smile or some nonverbal cue can say: "I'm proud of you for getting involved; do it again." Although no one else in the

group is aware that the hesitant member has been encouraged, he will know—with a warm heart-glow.

11. The leader stimulates critical thinking. One does not want the small-group situation to fall into a mutual admiration society or a "sweetness and light" atmosphere where honest doubts cannot be discussed. This is a major weakness in the church family. I have gone to prayer services where the rest of the people all exuberantly rejoiced in the Lord and *my* heart was like lead with problems I couldn't solve. Yet I would have been stared at with dismay had I honestly stated to that group my true feelings. The leader, to be his most effective, should do all in his power to avoid this.

Wouldn't it be great to form a Society of Thomas, where one is free to go with the tearing questions of his spirit, his doubts, his uncertainties, and have helpful Christian friends who would understand and assist him in finding Christ's answers? The Christian religion can stand probing questions. That is why it has survived almost 2,000 years. That is why when some of the greatest minds have attempted to tear down its tenets, they became Christian themselves and, instead of critiques, wrote masterpieces like *Ben Hur.*

Brilhart has given some techniques for encouraging critical thinking in a small-group situation:

a. Keep asking for information and analysis of the problem if the group gets solution minded.

b. See that evidence is tested for reliability and not accepted at face value. You might do this by asking questions which will encourage the group members to test and evaluate it. For example: "How does this apply to our [life] problem?" or "How is that like . . . situations we [face]?"

To evaluate the source of [an interpretation that has been cited], you might ask such questions as, "What is the source of that information?" "How well

58

is ——— recognized in his field?" "Is this consistent [with Christian doctrine as we understand it]?"

To check on the credibility of a [view cited], you might ask: "Do we have any information which is contradictory?"

c. See that all group members understand and evaluate all standards, criteria, or assumptions used in making value judgments. For example, you might ask, "Is that criterion clear to us all?" "Is this something we want to insist upon?" or "Do we all accept that as an assumption?"

d. See that all proposed solutions are given a thorough testing before they are accepted as group decisions.[1]

Don't accept the one interpretation or cliche that is most familiar to churchgoing people. Guide the small-group thinking into new areas. Not, certainly, that the cliche is untrue; it may be that, after full discussion, one comes back to it as fundamental truth. But not all commonly accepted tenets are conclusive or comprehensive. It could be that through open discussion you could find new ways of finding help from the Lord.

12. The leader stimulates creative thinking. Brilhart offers one way of encouraging creative thinking under the label of "Brainstorming." The rules of such activity he lists in this way:

a. All criticism is ruled out while brainstorming.

b. The wilder the ideas the better. Even offbeat, impractical suggestions may suggest practical ideas to other members.

c. Quantity is wanted. The more ideas, the more likelihood of good ones.

d. Combination and improvement are wanted. If you see a way to improve an idea, snap your fingers to get attention so it can be recorded at once.[2]

A full-time recorder will be necessary to take down

the ideas as fast as they are suggested. This can be done by tape, but it is better to have a visual record.

When attempting to stimulate creative thinking, Brilhart makes three other suggestions.

a. Apply the principle of deferred judgment even when not brainstorming, and try to get as many alternative solutions as possible. Perhaps you can use some of the following questions: "How *might* we ...?" (rather than "How *should* we ...?)" "What other ideas can we think of?" "Can we recall any solutions used elsewhere that might be used to help solve this problem [or give us some light on the application of this scripture to our lives]?"

b. An effective device is to take up each major characteristic of the problem and ask how it might be [interpreted, put in action, or internalized].

c. Watch for possible solutions which suggest whole new areas of thinking, and then pose a general question about the new area. [For example, if a member suggests that when Jesus says, "Love one another," He could specifically be implying, "Listen to one another." Perhaps the two are synonymous, so the leader might respond: "In what ways can listening be synonymous with loving? If so, how could we utilize this concept in improving our interpersonal relationships?"][3]

13. The leader strives to reduce the expression of ideas and judgments in biased, loaded, or emotive language. When someone responds: "That is a socialistic view," he should quickly rephrase the comment in words such as "You feel that this would bring too much government control?" By immediately defusing that loaded word "socialistic," the leader may lead the discussion along more rational lines. He must constantly be on the alert for rephrasing and discouraging the use of loaded words.

14. The leader uses questions effectively. It has often been said that "to know the right question is more important than knowing the right answer," and this is often true with the leader of small groups. The entire process of dialectic (a search for truth through dialogue) is a search for answers *to* questions. For this reason, the leader should always be equipped with questions to guide to answers. One helpful technique is simply to put forth the query: "What question are we now discussing?" An open statement of the question or issue and its implications will spotlight specificities and will often generate new areas of thought. Both *what* the leader asks and *how* he asks it are vital.

There are many kinds of questions a leader may use. Some basic ones are:

a. The *unanswerable* which simply produces stimulus for thought.

b. The *query for information* which asks for specific statements of fact.

c. The *query for interpretation or judgment* which asks for *meaning* of a fact or group of facts. This type of question stimulates discussion of implications.

d. The *query for value* which asks members to determine worth. A comparison is nearly always involved here.

e. The *query for policy* which asks what *should* be done. This deals with ideals and also sets up the potential for discussion of action to make that ideal a reality.

f. The *query for procedure* which is an assist in keeping the discussion organized and vague comments clarified.

g. The *query about goals* which is one that should be frequently used to remind the group of their *purposes* for meeting, for the discussion, for the life-help they are seeking.

h. The *query with rhetorical intent* which simply is

a tool which leads the discussion forward. An example is: "Wouldn't it be a good idea to brainstorm this question?"

i. The *close-ended question* which leaves no place for ongoing discussion because "yes" or "no'" suffice. This is often necessary when too much is being made of a certain point and the press of time necessitates moving on.

j. The *open-ended question* which stimulates. This not only works in the beginning of the discussion, but often follows on the heels of the close-ended question. It usually begins with "Why?" Examples: "Why did Jesus die on the Cross?" "Why is that significant in my life in the 20th century?"

k. The *people-interest query* which gets into a person's frame of reference and allows him to talk about what he wants to talk about. Examples: "Would you like to share what you are feeling right now?" "In relation to this concept, would you like to share how this applies to [circumstance of his life known to all]?"

l. The *question-answered query* which the leader uses to avoid having to answer a question himself. When asked a question that he knows another can answer, he simply relays the question to another discussant, thus keeping the dialogue going on between the group members rather than focusing on himself.

m. The *direct question* which is a head-on approach to a person whose needs keep getting into the conversation and you are *certain* that he would like to discuss a certain aspect of life or theology. Example: "Joe, how do you react to this?"

n. The *indirect question* is a general "overhead" question which anyone can answer. The group leader will use this often but, through eye contact with hesitant members, will hope for a more complete participation by all.

How the Leader Communicates

The leader of a small group is always communicating one way or another. He cannot be aloof. Even when he is not speaking, he communicates through the way he places his hands, the position of his body, his facial expression, etc. Lawrence Rosenfeld has done a study identifying specific elements which have been proven to form first impressions by members of group leaders. He states that after the impression of *physical characteristics* is the communication to every onlooker in regard to *apparel.* He cites a number of studies proving the significant relationship between the dress of an individual and his ability to lead. For example, Lefkowitz, Blake, and Mouton found that pedestrians were more likely to follow a well-dressed person (shined shoes, white shirt, tie, and freshly pressed suit) violating a pedestrian "wait" signal than one who was poorly dressed (worn shoes, soiled and patched pants, and blue denim shirt).[4] Consider the impression your apparel may make upon your leadership effectiveness.

Many studies have been done to prove that *facial expression* is a constant source of communication. Those who observe the leader's facial expressions will read his reactions, and you should be aware of this. Even if you do not reward or condemn verbally, you may do it through facial expression. Albeit an unconscious communication, it is still communication; and you must be aware of it and be sure that it communicates warmth, acceptance, and love, even in times of tension and conflict.

"How we stand and sit, the way we organize our bodies, may reveal something about how we feel."[5] Researchers have noted that eye contact, distance between the leader and the group, head orientation, leg orientation, shoulder orientation, arm and leg openness, and the degree of limb relaxation are all communication channels. "Results indicate that the more important variables for communicating positive attitude are a small backward lean of the torso, close distance, and great eye contact."[6]

Another factor that is nonverbal in essence is *vocal cues.* A study by Raymond Hunt and Tip Kan Lin concluded:

> The most noteworthy findings to emerge from this research are those that support the idea that stable cues to personality are carried by general voice "qualities" *independently of the lexical content* of speech. The fact that listeners could judge personality accurately from speech samples, but that passage content had no effect on accuracy, suggests either that speech content tends to be no more than redundant with voice quality or simply irrelevant to the judgmental task.[7]

In other words, no matter how "correct" the content of the leader's guidance, if his voice is abrasive, cold, or lacking in love, the content will be bypassed. But give to good content the warmth, glow, and kindness of a Christian spirit, and his nonverbal communication will enhance his words.

Another nonverbal factor of which a small-group leader should be aware is the concept of *personal space.* Rosenfeld has defined "personal space" as "the space carried around with you. Personal space is the space that you place between yourself and others, the invisible boundaries which become apparent only when they are crossed."[8] The average distance with strangers, in our culture, is about two feet. Sommers' study found that "two people prefer to sit across from one another, at a slight angle, rather than side-by-side, but, if the distance across is too great, they will prefer to sit side-by-side. A comfortable distance for conversation for people sitting across from each other is five and a half feet between heads (three and a half feet between couches)."[9] Another finding of Sommers is that people will arrange themselves around a *corner* of a table to facilitate discussion.

The leader of a small group should attempt to work in a comfortable "personal space" situation with his members, but never getting too close, never invading that "personal space" so there is any discomfort. He should try to arrange seating for everyone so that "personal space" is adequate for the kind of discussion that he is aiming for.

The leader's most personal and extensive symbol vocabulary is nonverbal, and is usually below the level of conscious awareness. That is why it is important to consider bringing it to the conscious level so that it works for him rather than, unwittingly, against him. Albert Mehrabian has stated that our nonverbal behavior *defines and determines the effectiveness and well-being* of our intimate, social, and working relationships. He goes on to assert: "In the realm of feelings, our facial expressions, postures, movements, and gestures are so important that when our words contradict the silent messages contained within them, others mistrust what we say—they rely almost completely on what we do."[10]

That is an awesome concept when one realizes that these are, so often, unconscious forms of communication; and yet many studies fully attest the old idiom: "What you are speaks so loudly I can't hear what you say."

Another concept which the small–group leader should internalize is that *every individual perceives the world differently.* Reality is a very "private" thing because everyone's view of the universe is different. Even identical twins have different life experiences, different people reactions, different physiologies, etc. This puts an added burden on communication. Edward Rintyre has stated that "individual perception is a function of a person's biology, cultural training, and personal psychology."[11] There is no true "average" human being. All people are biologically different, an example being the married couple who spend nighttime turning electric blanket thermostats. Mead has stated that reality is "a transaction between an individual and the 'world out there.'"[12] It seems a point of substance.

A second point Rintyre feels a small-group leader should consider is that our *culture attempts to "socialize" us to particular values* and ways of behaving. So in addition to biological constraints that vary from individual to individual, so is the distortion of one's personal cultural conditioning.

Rintyre's third point of emphasis is *one's own individual psychology.* "Literally, 'psychology' refers to the logic of the mind or psyche of a person, and this is the framework with which he perceives the world. In effect, each individual has a uniquely tinted pair of glasses, through which he views life, and the basic point of reference which determines what he sees is his 'self-concept.' Self-concept is a kind of 'psychological base of operations.'"[13] S. I. Hayakawa succinctly summarizes that the "self-concept is *the* fundamental determinant of our perceptions, and therefore of our behavior." What the group leader must learn from this is that *the need to defend our self-concept* is among the most potent of all needs. This is the reason for the stress made so far on sensitivity to the feelings of others, making others feel accepted and carefully listened to even when they are not in tune with Christian doctrine. A member must never feel condemned or rejected because of a stated idea.

Rintyre has written:

> It is response to perceived threat [to our self-concept] that we most immediately, vigorously, and predictably "adjust" our perceptions to maintain self-esteem and self-regard. [As many studies have suggested], behavior which is perceived as threatening inevitably results in restriction of the "victim's" perceptual field. It is not necessary that a genuine threat exists or is intended, only that behavior "out there" is perceived as threatening. Defensive responses inhibit accurate perception, obviously, and greatly interfere with the communication process. On the other hand, when a person feels accepted and supported by what he perceives, his perceptual field broadens, his communication accuracy increases, and his willingness to be open and honest expands.[14]

The implications of this response pattern to threat versus support are of great importance to the one who wants to most effectively lead small groups within the church structure. How to achieve that insight is our initial challenge. Once this is perceived, to move with humility, patience, and perseverance in groundwork is a never-ending goal. Probably the key is to try to refrain from going through ritual motions of communication and taking the time to function with people *where they are* with *what we know.*

Confidence and trust must be developed among group members themselves and with the leader if the small group is to be its most effective for God. Ultimately, open sharing of personal problems should be a goal. As this is done, and the leadership of the Holy Spirit is realized, it should be very much in order, in fact *natural,* to pray about needs under discussion right then—whether it is a problem or blessing. In reality, natural prayer should be as common a part of the ideal small group as any other aspect of sharing. Prayer becomes more meaningful, and confidence and trust are stimulated between the children of God and with their Heavenly Father. Thus the vertical/horizontal, God/man relationship is at its best. Conversational prayer is, perhaps, the most meaningful way to lead those who have never prayed aloud before. Rosalind Rinker's book, *Conversational Prayer*, may be one that you will recommend for group reading.

6

The Techniques of Leadership

Christ's injunction: "Ask, and it shall be given you; seek, and ye shall find; knock, and it shall be opened unto you" (Matt. 7:7), is the key to learning in the small-group situation. The *togetherness* of seeking is vital. The group leader is responsible, in the main, for the generation of that intangible feeling of togetherness, as "sons and daughters" of the Heavenly Father.

Without doubt, the most important meeting for the small group is the first. It will be handled this time differently from the more structured time-adhered-to meetings that will come later. There are three major steps to consider in this first meeting.

1. Get acquainted with one another so honest discussion and interaction can take place *from the beginning.* As each person arrives, introduce him to the others. To help the people remember each other's names, call

each person by name as often as possible. If necessary, name tags can be used.

Help the members of the group to get to know one another by having each person share something about himself. Start with general impersonal questions: hometown; occupation; hobbies; etc. The leader should share first. That will break the ice. Include anecdotes in your presentation to include embarrassing moments, funny incidents, etc., so that laughter will result, people will identify with your humanity, and ease will begin to slide into the atmosphere. This will also set a precedent which others may follow as they choose.

Asking unusual even though unimportant questions can add some humor and help everyone relax. Instead of relying on "top of the head" inspiration, you might make cards with different questions, place in a bowl, and have one draw a question to answer in the course of their self-introduction. Here are some examples:

> Who was your fourth grade teacher? What did she look like?
> What qualities do you like best in a cookie?
> What do you like to do best on a rainy day?

When the group is comprised of Christians only, you could ask for a testimony-sharing time. If you are using the small group for outreach, and there are those present without testimony, delete that part of the get-acquainted format. Never place a member in a position of feeling uncomfortable for any reason.

2. Ask everyone to bow for prayer. You may want to begin with the focus in the first chapter of the book which dealt with God's promise that we are all His sons and daughters and that "where two or three are gathered" in His name, He would be there to talk with them. Ask that God guide each phase of discussion of His be-

70

loved children and help them to hear His voice giving guidance through Scripture, through human love-channels, and through inner insights.

3. You may now want to present copies of the purposes and scriptures set forth in the beginning of this book to read together now and to have in participants' hands for further perusal. You may also want to have an organized schedule of your plans as to what you will be studying, when, and how. If you have books or other materials, present them now. If printed matter is being used, be sure to go over the introduction and instructions carefully. To assist in holding attention, have members take turns reading a paragraph at a time of anything lengthy. Voice change helps attention span. Stop and discuss what has been read whenever it seems necessary.

4. Immediately launch into the study. There should be a sense of expectancy in the group. This will mainly be initiated by the leader. Norman Vincent Peale wrote a book on "Enthusiasm" which everyone should read. If you are excited about the possibilities of God-venturing in the small group, it will be contagious. Every time.

5. As your hour draws to a close, conclude with prayer. As you adjourn for the fellowship time, remind everyone of the time of the next meeting and the assignment for the next study. If you have budgeted your time carefully, each of the three steps mentioned here should take about one-third of your time of this opening session. After this, you will, as already stated, begin work immediately and continue for an hour. Then comes the half-hour of fellowship.

As you begin your work as group leader, you need to be aware that there are several types of observed small-group communication networks that can emerge. Because this is something that you can control, you should consider these findings and choose to deliberately

71

create the one that you feel has the best potential for making your small group most effective.

Brilhart mentions four basic ones.[1]

1. The Wheel Communication Network

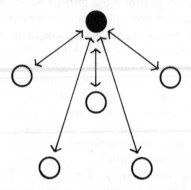

The wheel network is so called because almost all talking is done to one member. A dominating small-group leader will produce this pattern if he insists that all persons be recognized by him before they speak, if he restates comments, asks all the questions, and generally controls all participation. While this pattern is efficient and less time-consuming in arriving at solutions to problems presented, it tends to reduce personal questing, breed dependency on the leader, and lower group cohesiveness. If people want to hear a sermon, they can go to the sanctuary. If they want to go to a lecture, they can go to Sunday School. But when they want to share with each other in *interaction,* they go to small groups.

2. A Hierarchical Communication Network

Brilhart states that "in one form of subgrouping, two or more relatively low-power members interact with a

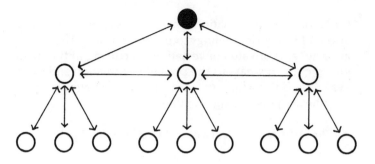

higher power member, but not with each other. The high power members interact with each other, but not with the members of each other's subgroups."[2] The high power members are the only ones to interact with the top man or central leader. Such a pattern, as can quickly be seen, indicates a split in the subgroup goals, taking priority over the common purpose of the meeting.

3. The Private Conversation Communication Network

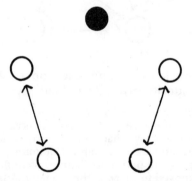

This common form of subgrouping within a larger group involves two or more private conversations which occur in the situation. Such conversations take some members out of the discussion. The whispering or low tones of the conversations may be distracting and may also add insecurity feelings to other members. The entire allowance of private conversations occurring in the small group context weakens the pool of information and ideas available to the whole group and badly damages feelings of cohesiveness among members.

4. The All-Channel Network of Communication

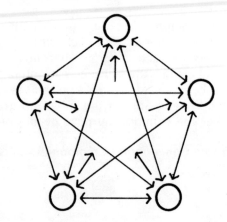

This is the kind of communication network for which you would ideally strive. As Brilhart says:

> It permits rapid communication without getting clearance from a central authority. Everyone is free to speak up and say what he has to say while it is still pertinent and fresh in mind. Communication flows freely from one person to another, according to whoever is moved to speak at the moment. Attention will shift frequently and quite at random from person-to-person. Most of the comments will be directed to the group as a whole, rather than to individual members. Such group-centered comments tend to keep the channels of communication open to everyone, en-

couraging any and all to speak, and permitting free feedback of questions and answers among all members. Many studies have shown morale to be highest in an all-channel network. Departures from this pattern should be relatively brief.[3]

Thomas Gordon has listed the rewards of the all-channel network as six in number:

First, group members will feel that their contributions are of sufficient worth to merit being listened to and understood by the leader. This should greatly facilitate participation by the members through reduction of the threat of devaluation.

Second, group members will make a greater effort to express their ideas and opinions more clearly, knowing that someone in the group is listening attentively and is going to reflect their ideas back to them for confirmation.

Third, group members will begin to drop their defensiveness, open their minds to new understandings, think more flexibly, reason more effectively. This should not only improve the quality of contributions, but increase the problem-solving ability of the group as a whole.

Fourth, when conflicts or controversies arise in the group, each member is more likely to alter his own point of view rather than defend it vigorously and stubbornly.

Fifth, group members observing that the leader is listening with understanding will, themselves, begin to listen to each other more attentively and with more understanding.

Sixth, the leader himself will learn far more from listening to others in the group than he would through giving lectures, presentations, and other leader-centered activities.

The all-channel network contributes significantly to the small group's long-range objectives and goals— (1) creating a nonthreatening group atmosphere conducive to creative participation by the members, and (2) facilitating communication so that the various members' contributions will be understood by the others and utilized by the group.[4]

Small-group communication is a process of having the give-and-take that characterizes people working together. Examination of a unit of communication indicates the basic parts and how they fit together. Once the components are clearly identified and described, one can set them in motion to see how the process works.

Although this book is aimed primarily for the small-group leader within the church structure, it may be well to ask some members of the group to assist in specific ways. This is especially true if the group is organized with other Christians within its membership. Whether or not there is such a recruitment, it may be helpful to look at a list of "Group Task Roles" which could be discussed with key participants and they be encouraged to assume certain roles in discussion. If there are people working to fulfill these functions, there will be a more continual flow of information, ideas, and energy necessary for the group to accomplish its job. This will lead more clearly to the All-Channel Network which should also be shared with key members as your ideal goal of interaction.

Brilhart lists these roles as follows:

1. Initiator—proposes new ideas, new goals, procedures, methods, solutions
2. Information seeker—asks for facts, clarification or information from other members, or suggests information is needed before making decisions
3. Opinion seeker—draws out convictions and opinions of others, asks for clarification of position or values involved
4. Opinion giver—states own belief or opinion, expresses a judgment
5. Information giver—offers facts and information,

76

personal experiences and evidence (note that information is useful to accomplishing the task only when it is both pertinent and valid)

6. Clarifier—elaborates on ideas expressed by another, often by giving an example, illustration or explanation
7. Coordinator—clarifies relationships among facts, ideas, and suggestions, or suggests an integration of ideas and activities of two or more members
8. Orienter—clarifies purpose or goal, defines position of the group, summarizes or suggests the direction of the discussion
9. Energizer—prods group to greater activity or to a decision, stimulates activity, or warns of need to act while still time
10. Procedure developer—offers suggestions for accomplishing ideas of others, or handles such tasks as seating arrangements, running the projector, passing out papers and so forth
11. Recorder—keeps written record on paper, chart or blackboard, serving as group's "memory"

Group Building and Maintenance Roles
These behaviors establish and maintain cooperative interpersonal relationships and a group-centered orientation.

1. Supporter—praises, agrees, indicates warmth and solidarity with others or goes along with them
2. Harmonizer—mediates differences between others, reconciles disagreement, conciliates
3. Tension reliever—jokes or brings out humor in a situation, reduces formality and status differences, relaxes others
4. Gatekeeper—opens channels of communication, brings in members who otherwise might not speak, sees that all have equitable chance to be heard[5]

If you have people who can be in supportive roles with you in the small-group situation, it will increase the chances of fully meeting your group goals. It is very difficult for the communication in a small group to work well unless thought and planning go into its organization. It is not simply a matter of people getting together and letting it "happen." Communication is too complex for that. Lewis Carroll points out an example of such behavior—everybody "doing his thing" with no thought of the problems of communication—in his delightfully insightful discussion between Alice and Humpty Dumpty:

> "I don't know what you mean by 'glory,'" Alice said.
> Humpty Dumpty smiled contemptuously. "Of course you don't till I tell you. I meant 'there's a nice knockdown argument for you!'"
> "But 'glory' doesn't mean 'a nice knockdown argument,'" Alice objected.
> "When I use a word," Humpty Dumpty said, in rather a scornful tone, "it means just what I choose it to mean—neither more nor less."
> "The question is," said Alice, "whether you *can* make words mean so many different things."
> "The question is," said Humpty Dumpty, "which is to be master—that's all."[6]

As Humpty Dumpty cogently points out: Meanings of words are *in* people. An oft-repeated idiom is: "Words don't mean; people do!" Nowhere is that more crucial than in the interchange of ideas through words in a small group. The better trained that the leader of the group can be, the better trained his key members can be, the better the chances for purpose fulfillment. Effective small groups don't just happen; they are created with prayer, study, organization, selflessness, caring, and pure hard work on the part of the leader.

Important Techniques of Leadership

1. Identification

Kenneth Burke, in dealing with this technique of effective leadership, wrote: "You can persuade a man only in so far as you can talk his language by speech, gesture, tonality, order, image, attitude, idea, *identifying your ways with his.*"[7] In other words, identification can be succinctly defined as "establishing common ground."

There are four basic areas of identification: interests, feelings, beliefs, and methods.

a. Interests

Mutual interests form a strong bond. This forms a bridge over which any man can walk regardless of how diversified the other person's stand on a particular issue may be. It was through the shared interest with my wife in creative writing that an atheist graduate student joined a small Bible study group in our home when we were at the university. Because they were bonded in a common interest, she was curious to have the group experience. It led to her conversion.

b. Feelings

People are much more similar emotionally than they are intellectually. All feel fear, hatred, love, patriotism, loyalty, duty, humor, excitement. When a leader can help a group to feel bonded in the universals of emotion, there is a cohesiveness that will withstand the onslaught of diverse ideas.

c. Beliefs

James Albert Winans, in his textbook *Speech Making,* set forth the ideal in this succinct bit of dialogue between two persons who had a problem between them.

Said the first: "Well, let's talk over our points of difference." "No," said the other, "let's talk over our points
of agreement." In many small groups I am involved with,
the strain of Calvinism is very strong. Were I to focus on
this, there would be a spirit of divisiveness, little learning
could occur, and ultimately people would leave the
group. We have to continually highlight together our
points of agreement and then work, as we may, on the
points of disagreement which take time to solve.

d. Methods

"Let's do it your way" is a good mental approach
for a leader to carry to his group. Every game has its rules,
and every unruly player is considered a nuisance by the
others. But he *is* valuable.

Henry Ward Beecher, in his third lecture to the Yale
Divinity students, gave to these young people precisely
this fruit of his long and successful preaching experience:

> Now, in order to reach and help all these varying
> phrases of your congregation, you must take human
> nature as you find it, in its broad range. Understand
> this, that the same law that led the Apostle to make
> himself a Greek to the Greeks, and a Jew to the Jews,
> and to put himself under the law with those who were
> under the law; and that same everlasting good sense
> of conformity in these things, for the sake of taking
> hold of men where they can be reached, and lifting
> them up, requires you to study human nature *as it
> is,* and not as people tell you it ought to be.
>
> If a man can be saved by pure intellectual preach-
> ing, let him have it. If others require a predominance
> of emotion, provide that for them. If, by others, the
> Truth is taken more easily through the imagination,
> give it to them in forms attractive to the imagination.
> If there are still others who demand it in the form of
> facts and rules, see that they have it in that form. Take
> men as it has pleased God to make them; and let your
> preaching so far as it concerns the selection of ma-

terial, and the mode and method by which you are presenting the Truth, follow the wants of the persons themselves, and not simply the measure of your own minds.[8]

As you develop methods for leading a small group, strive to incorporate the following:

1) Stress the obvious touchstones of identification that you have with other members.

2) Stress any basic agreement of goals (personal, family, social, group, church, country, world, etc.).

3) Stress any basic agreement on fundamental beliefs. I remember a lady in a small group in one of my churches who came to her neighbor's house. She believed in the deity of Christ, but that was the only significant point on which we agreed. But when she tended to become angered at the doctrine presented in the small-group study, I would remind her (teasingly) that she would be willing to give me a hearing because I was intelligent enough to agree with her on *one* point. She would laugh, smooth her "feathers," and listen. It took two years, but she is a thoroughly indoctrinated church-woman today. The key to her activity for God now was held on the one point of identification with *one* basic belief.

4) Strive to keep the member's attention focused on major issues rather than peripheral differences.

5) Work toward your chosen conclusion, but attempt to do it by means of the group members' specific line of reasoning (which may vary greatly with each group).

In one of my churches, I had two small-group Bible studies back-to-back. In the driving time from one house to the other, I had to totally shift mental gears. I would be covering the same material; I had the same goal; but the groups were so diverse that I had to radically revamp each step of my approach.

6) Avoid carefully any appearance of dogmatism. Flexibility is always the best way to work with people. Being willing to listen openly will help you see how you can state your doctrinal position without having head-on collisions.

7) Be willing to identify with your group by sharing your own human weaknesses and needs. It is difficult to relate to a "super Christian." In the small-group setting, identification is a major touchstone in the horizontal understanding of what it is like to be human!

8) Stress Jesus' *identification* with man. In a play written by my wife, Ruth, she has one bit of dialogue that underscores this point:

> His death, on the Center Cross of Golgotha, enabled Jesus of Nazareth, the God-man to internalize human experience totally: all the senselessness ... all the anguish ... all the frustration ... all the fear. The God-man, on that Center Cross, experienced *for himself* the heart-ripping despair of human loneliness, alienation, and desertion. The Man on the Center Cross called from the pain-quivering chasm of His soul the human shriek of despondency ... abandonment . . . and betrayal: *"My God, my God, why hast thou forsaken me?"* And, in that moment, He had internalized the broad spectrum of human existence.[9]

2. Affirmation

Affirmation is what happens when you and I see each other as valuable and worthwhile and when we communicate this perception to each other. Affirmation is simply communicating to another person: "You are important. You are cared about!"

In our depersonalized culture, this is one of the greatest human needs. Each person has to believe that he is *important*. Psychologists say that the most critical need of people today is for improved self-image, improved self-knowledge, and improved self/others relationships. To this should be added the need for dynamic God/man relations. This last is the point of the small group within the church.

It may be helpful to take a look at what is called the "Johari Window." Developed by Joseph Luft,[10] it is a device for speculating about human relations.

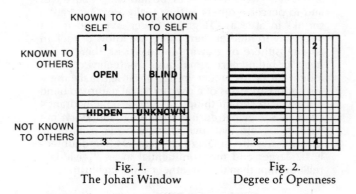

<table>
<tr><td></td><td>KNOWN TO SELF</td><td>NOT KNOWN TO SELF</td></tr>
</table>

Fig. 1.
The Johari Window

Fig. 2.
Degree of Openness

The explanation of the four quadrants:

Quadrant 1, the area of free activity, or open area, refers to behavior and motivation known to self and known to others.

Quadrant 2, the blind area is where others can see things in ourselves of which we are unaware (e.g., cultism or prejudice).

Quadrant 3, the avoided or hidden area, represents things we know but do not reveal to others (e.g., a hidden agenda or matters about which we have sensitive feelings).

Quadrant 4, the area of unknown activity, points to the area where neither the individual nor others are aware of certain behaviors or motives. Yet we can assume their existence because eventually some of these things become known, and we then realize that these unknown behaviors and motives were influencing relationships all along.[11]

Figure 2 pictures the effects of a small group upon each individual's "Johari Window," which Luft describes as follows:

> In a new group Q1 is very small; there is not much free and spontaneous interaction. As the group grows and matures, Q1 expands in size, and this usually means we are freer to be more like ourselves and to perceive others as they really are. Quadrant 3 shrinks in area as Q1 grows larger. We find it less necessary to hide or deny things we know or feel. In an atmosphere of growing mutual trust, there is less need for hiding pertinent thoughts or feelings. It takes longer for Q2 to reduce in size because usually there are "good" reasons of a psychological nature to blind ourselves to certain things we feel or do. Quadrant 4 changes somewhat during a learning laboratory, but we can assume that such changes occur even more slowly than shifts in Q2. At any rate, Q4 is undoubtedly far larger and more influential in an individual's relationships than the hypothetical sketch illustrates.[12]

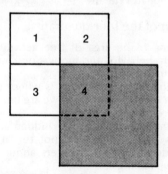

Fig. 3.
The relative size of Q4.

Of course, the best means of changing self-image and increasing all four quadrants of understanding is to have a personal knowledge of and experience with God.

"Thou shalt call me, My father" (Jer. 3:19).

"God is love" (1 John 4:8).

"Under this new plan we have been forgiven and made clean by Christ's dying for us once and for all" (Heb. 10:10, TLB).

"The Lord your God is with you wherever you go" (Josh. 1:9, TLB).

"When we obey him, every path he guides us on is fragrant with his lovingkindness and his truth" (Ps. 25:10, TLB).

"I was my father's [child], tender and only beloved" (Prov. 4:3).

The power of those scriptures alone can transform self-image and begin to widen those quadrants of self-knowledge. The Creator not only made each person; He has full knowledge of all the effects of life upon personality. He understands Quadrant 4 in totality, and self-image will rise when one understands: I am my Father's child, "tender and only beloved." That loving Heavenly Father will forgive sins and lead along the paths that one should follow.

Self-understanding has to come in a supernatural transformation by the Holy Spirit and the guidance of an all-wise God. "These things I plan won't happen right away. Slowly, steadily, surely, the time approaches when the vision will be fulfilled. If it seems slow, do not despair, for these things will surely come to pass. Just be patient!" (Hab. 2:3, TLB).

That scripture is not only excellent exhortation for the group members striving to increase self-understanding with God. It is also excellent exhortation for the group leader. The effects of life's scars remain even after the new birth and the coming of the Holy Spirit. Many personality "warts" still have to be worked on with God. It takes time; so be patient!

In addition to God's working to broaden self-concept, self-understanding, and reduce the blind and hidden-self areas, He can move through the leader, as a channel, in many ways. A vital element of his ministry is to be used for this very purpose. One of the most important things people can do is to *affirm* one another; say and demonstrate to each other that they are *loved!*

As a person experiences being loved and valued within the small group, God brings the truth of His words to life; and with that *reality,* it is easier for the person to change. In small groups, we should focus on knowing each other as we are, and showing in compelling ways that each is loved and valued—as he is.

What are some ways that this communication can take place?

a. *Listen.* Listening carefully says: You are important; your ideas, even if diverse from mine, are important; I care about you enough to try to find out *what it is like to be you!*

b. *Share.* In allowing another to know of your heartaches, your fears, your struggles, a bond is formed. You affirm him by trusting him enough to share.

c. *Accept him as he is.* Remember, you are not the one who can convert his soul, change his life, or solve his problems. That is God's work. But you can hold his hand, in caring love, while he struggles and seeks to find, know, and understand God. You can welcome him with no changes asked. Some small groups have a "price" of admission: that each one agree to all doctrinal tenets precious to the group leader and the key members. That small group usually remains "holy" but *small!*

d. "Bear . . . one another's burdens" (Gal. 6:2).

e. "Provoke unto love and to good works" (Heb. 10:24). The RSV translates this: "Let us consider how to stir up one another to love and good works." This is a ministry of affirming one another by showing both trust and expectation. As Christians, we may expect God to be working *in* us—and working *through* us. If we are doing our best vertically, we should be expecting Him to be changing us. If we are doing our best horizontally, He should be working through us to encourage and stir up others to act in faith and confidence that God will supply all needs.

3. Single Focus

We have already established that the *purpose* of the small group within the church structure is *ministry*. Although everything discussed here is important to the most complete fulfilling of that purpose, the vital element is that the focus of every bit of discussion be upon the Father God himself as revealed to us in Jesus Christ. Whenever this becomes peripheral, the goal begins to disintegrate.

To the Christian, the Bible is God's revelation to man of himself, of His character, and of His willingness and desire to work with His creation. On that basis rests our ability to distinguish reality from illusion.

To the Christian, Jesus Christ is God. The prevalent thesis of our intellectual age is that Jesus was a great moral teacher on a par with Buddha and Ghandi. If this idea is ever expressed in the group, the leader should respond with the succinct statement of C. S. Lewis in *The Case for Christianity:*

> I am trying to prevent anyone from saying the really silly thing that people often say about Him:

"I'm ready to accept Jesus as a great moral teacher, but I don't accept his claim to be God." That's the one thing we mustn't say. A man who was merely a man and said the sort of things Jesus said wouldn't be a great moral teacher. He'd be either a lunatic— on a level with a man who says he's a poached egg— or else he'd be the Devil of hell. You must make your choice. Either this man was, and is, the Son of God, or else a madman or something worse. You can shut Him up for a fool, you can spit at Him and kill Him for a demon; or you can fall at His feet and call Him Lord and God. But don't let us come up with any patronizing nonsense about His being a great human teacher. He hasn't left that open to us.[13]

When there are members in your group who have still not made these choices, suggest that, in their home, they read C. S. Lewis and others who argue cogently the intellectual presentation of the deity of Christ and the inerrancy of the Bible. The mind *is* a door to God. The other door is the one of personal experience. Invite the uncommitted group members to participate in the discussions, in the prayers, and in the heart-sharing in a state of openness. If they will do that, they will come to know God through the second door which is truly more life-transforming than the first.

The following poem can open the door to a personal experience with God in a unique way.

>*God, I need to talk!*
>*Are You there?*
>
>*"I shall never leave*
>*you nor forsake you."*
>
>*"I am with you always."*
>
>*God, I need to talk!*
>*Will You listen?*

*"I will hear your prayers
and answer them. I will
bend down and listen."*

*"I will listen to your
troubles and see the
crisis in your soul."*

*God, I need to talk!
Will You talk back?*

*"Listen and I will speak.
Let me put the questions
to you! See if you can
answer them!"*

*"O my child, listen!
For I am your God.
Listen . . . I want your
promises fulfilled.
I want you to trust me
in your times of trouble,
so I can rescue you, and
you can give me glory."*[14]

As has been stated, the most meaningful door to invite people into the fellowship of the group is the door of personal experience. Charles Colson, in his book, *Born Again,* tells of a time when, as an avowed atheist, in a moment with his son, his heart completely bypassed his mental reasoning and he dialogued with God. Later he did work in the intellectual process of acceptance. But he never forgot that *experience* of intuitively knowing and feeling the presence of God.

Encourage these people to be a part of the group dynamics, but be very careful that you always keep the central focus on God and upon His Word. Stress the fact that the Bible is not just for *learning;* it is for *living.* The

Bible reveals a reality that we can experience if we will open ourselves to it. The Bible challenges us (even the well-indoctrinated churchmen) to literally believe God's promises that His own power and His own life will actually enter, control, and enable us to do exceeding and abundantly beyond our natural abilities.

The specific functions of the Bible in the small-group situation has been summarized this way by Lawrence O. Richards:

> 1. The Bible is explored for light and truth. We know that God's revelation gives us an accurate picture of every reality we need to understand. We come to see God as He is; we come to understand ourselves; we discover how we may live to please God and experience His joy and love....
>
> 2. The Bible is for living, not simply for learning. God's objective revelation of truth is always to be explored in view of its impact on human experience. Here a group study makes a unique contribution. When each person shared, "Here's how I see this truth affecting my life," our vision expands. The Holy Spirit works through each of us to illumine and make clear the *meaning to me* of what God has said to us all....
>
> It is vital that whenever the Bible is studied, we move together from "What is revealed" to state clearly "What this means to me."
>
> 3. The Word is to be experienced. This last element simply means that we are to *do* what we've seen in Scripture. We are to obey, to "continue in" Christ's words, to "keep My words."[15]

Keep the focus of the small group constantly upon God who will not only redeem us from our sins but enable us to make creative use of all circumstances of our lives. It is He who said: "I am the Lord your God, who ...leads you along the paths that you should follow" (Isa. 48:17, TLB).

Helpful Tools in the Small Group

1. Various recent translations of the Bible will help facilitate comprehension.

2. A comprehensive dictionary for precise definitions

3. Commentaries, especially the one-volume kind that are easy to handle and carry

4. Newspaper, magazine, or other source materials that illustrate biblical principles—not only anecdotes, reports, stories, but even pictures and cartoons. (Charlie Brown often explicitly defines scriptural truth.)

5. Charts, graphs, posters, models, artwork, etc.

7

Problems in Leadership

As diagrammed and discussed in an earlier chapter, what we propose to do in a small group is to develop communication between people. This is a complex task. It includes the linguistic level, the physiological level, and the acoustic level. And all of these must function correctly between speaker and listeners if there is to be effective communication. It cannot be blithely taken for granted that when people sit down together to discuss, that true sharing will occur even though all are well intentioned. Communication can break down at any of many points. Consider such problems as these:

1. The idea may be "fuzzy"; that is, the speaker may not have adequate, clear information.

2. The message may not be expressed in accurate, effective, transmittable words.

3. Noise (any interference with transmission) may obscure all, most, or some of the message, so that the speaker's message may not be the one received by the

decoder. The speaker may speak too softly to be heard. Someone in the audience may cough.

4. The message may be heard accurately, but may not mean the same thing to the listener as to the speaker. At the receiver's end, "noise" can be misinterpretation resulting from the listener's biases and emotions or his lack of information.

The group represents the accumulated experiences, emotions, and motivations of the people trying to communicate. The source (speaker) can encode and the destination (listener) can decode *only* in terms of his experience. If we have never learned any German, we can neither encode nor decode in that language. If a South African tribesman has neither seen nor heard of television, he can only decode the sight of a television set in terms of whatever experience he has had. If there is no common experience, then communication is impossible. If there is only a small area in common, then it will be very difficult for the speaker to convey his intended meaning to the audience.[1]

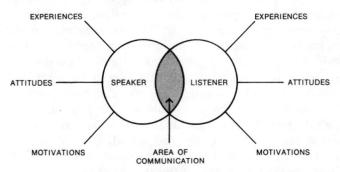

Because we understand the complexity of the communication process, the small-group leader should be aware of specific, identifiable problems that will arise. Some of these are:

1. Bypassing

This problem stems from the erroneous belief that the image in my mind when I use a word will be the same in your mind when you hear the word. *Meaning resides in the user of the word.* That is what must be deeply internalized.

An example of this occurred in my first pastorate. My family was invited to a lovely lady's home for "dinner." Having grown up in the South, we ate breakfast, dinner, and supper. Having grown up in the East, the lovely lady ate breakfast, lunch, and dinner.

You know the result, don't you? My family arrived at 12:00 to find the lovely lady with curlers in her hair, dust mop in hand, and bathrobe covering. We were all mortified. Why? We had bypassed each other's meaning. Each of us had assumed that the common word *dinner* evoked the same meaning in us all. That it did not, sent the lovely lady into an almost hysterical state and the minister's family into red-faced, hurried departure.

Not all bypassing is so trivial. Bypassings daily result in enormous wastes of emotion, effort, time, marital harmony, job harmony, etc. History contains prolific examples of bypassing leading to catastrophe.[2] There is even strong suggestion that bypassing on a word in the Japanese response to the World War II Potsdam ultimatum may have directly been the cause of dropping the atomic bombs on Hiroshima and Nagasaki, and Russia's declaration of war on Japan—events which have had irreparable influence on the world. (See William J. Coughlin, "Was It the Deadliest Error of Our Time?" *Harper's Magazine,* March, 1953).

One of the reasons for bypassing is that we *want* to be understood. We *want* so much to be "family" that everyone eats "dinner" at noon!

A second reason is our egocentrism pointed up in the quote earlier used about Humpty Dumpty telling Alice: "When I use a word, it means just what I choose it to mean, neither more nor less."[3] Few of us want to admit to that arrogance, but it *is* a human trait.

A third reason is that we have the fallacy that words have only one definition. We know better, but in conversation, we usually forget that other definitions of the same term exist. William Haney highlights this:

A person is *fast* when he can run rapidly.
But he is also *fast* when he is tied down and cannot run at all.
And colors are *fast* when they do not run.
One is *fast* when he moves in suspect company.
But this is not quite the same thing as playing *fast* and loose.
A racetrack is *fast* when it is in good running condition.
A friend is *fast* when he is loyal.
A watch is *fast* when it is ahead of time.
To be *fast* alseep is to be deep in sleep.
To be *fast* by is to be near.
To *fast* is to refrain from eating.
A *fast* may be a period of noneating—or a ship's mooring line.
Photographic film is *fast* when it is sensitive (to light).
But bacteria are *fast* when they are insensitive (to antiseptics).[4]

A fourth reason is the constant changing of definition in the coining of new words, the individual lingo each generation of teenagers creates, phrases meaningful in certain media shows which are watched by many, but not everyone. An anonymous poet summed it up like this.

Remember when hippie meant big in the hips,
And a trip involved travel in cars, planes and ships?
When pot was a vessel for cooking things in,
And hooked was what grandmother's rugs may have been?

95

When fix was a verb that meant mend or repair,
And be-in meant merely existing somewhere?
When neat meant well-organized, tidy and clean,
And grass was a ground cover, normally green?
When groovy meant furrowed with channels and
*   hollows,*
And birds were winged creatures, like robins and
*   swallows?*
When fuzz was a substance, real fluffy, like lint,
And bread came from bakeries and not from the
*   mint?*
When roll meant a bun, and rock was a stone,
And hang-up was something you did with the phone?
It's groovy, man, groovy, but English it's not.
Methinks that our language is going to pot.[5]

Another reason for bypassing is the regional differences of language.

Augustine understood the problem of bypassing almost 15 centuries ago when, in *Christian Instruction,* he wrote that words do not have intrinsic meaning. "Rather, they 'have' a meaning because men agreed upon them." The current rephrasing of that is: *Words don't mean: people do!* We must face the fact that most of us place our personal definitions on the words we hear.

Haney has offered four correctives which the leader of a small group may follow:

a. *Be person-minded, not word-minded*

The leader frequently asks himself: This is what it means to *me,* but what does it, or will it, mean to *him?* What would I mean if I were in *his* position? Does my interpretation of his words coincide with his viewpoint (as I see it)? Are the sender and receiver fixing the variables the same way?

b. *Query and paraphrase*

Ask questions when you don't understand or can't make sense out of what you heard. Ask questions when you think there may be a legitimate interpretation other than the one which first occurred to you. Paraphrase when you sense something out of alignment—something which doesn't quite mesh with the rest of your knowledge of a situation.

c. *Be approachable*

Do my group members feel free to query, paraphrase, and, in general, communicate up to me? Have I done everything possible to make their channel to me free and clear—and do I keep it that way? Do I make an extra effort to be approachable to more timid, reticent people? Am I genuinely receptive to feedback and do I continuously communicate my receptivity to others?

d. *Be sensitive to contexts*

Webster defines context: the part or parts of a written or spoken passage preceding or following a particular word or groups of words and so intimately associated with them as to throw light upon their meaning [verbal context]; . . . the interrelated conditions in which something exists or occurs [situational context of the small group].[6]

2. Allness

This is the common communication barrier where a person has the mental attitude that he knows *everything* about a subject, and speaks up accordingly. "I have never seen that done." (It follows, of course, that *that* cannot be done!) "I have never heard of that." (It follows, of course, that *that* does not exist.)

Group discussion is intended to widen knowledge horizons. The person who assumes allness does not even understand this *need*. People who have grown up in the church tend to have this feeling that they know all about the Bible, all about God and His dealings with men, particularly when they are with a group of people who are new in the faith. They need to realize that no matter how long one has been a Christian, how studious his study, one is always *becoming*.

I like Haney's diagram of the defeating power of all-ness in the life of any person's inner growth.

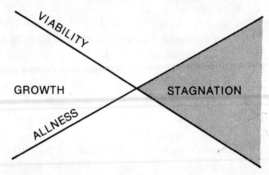

When one's *viability* is high, his *allness* is correspondingly low. As allness increases, the viability decreases and the growth potential diminishes.[7]

The best corrective for allness is humility. Be aware, and encourage in your members the awareness that no one knows *all* about anything. Constantly be checking yourself: "Do I have an 'all-wall'?" If so, break it down. If you see an "all-wall" operating in your group, try to find ways to dissolve it.

3. Indiscrimination

This communication barrier may be defined as "the neglect of differences while over-emphasizing similarities."[8] Classifying and categorizing are important to get along in a complex world. But to do so brings on many problems in understanding. I had two group members who found it impossible to communicate because of indiscrimination. The older gentleman lumped all long-haired young males into a group called "Yippies," who were then highly visible in media coverage. Because of the *similarities* in dress and hair length of some of the youth who came to our discussion, the gentleman became almost violent. He could never believe, for an instant, that the philosophy of this young man might be different from other young men whose dress and hair style were *similar* to his. I finally had to place the two men in different groups. They found it impossible to communicate. Neither could understand that surface similarity did not automatically indicate mental and spiritual similarity.

The basic corrective for indiscrimination is an intensive focus on differences. There is no identicalness in the universe—not in snowflakes; not in flowers; not even in twins; certainly not in groups. All stereotyping and prejudices arise because people refuse to look for the uniqueness that is present in *all* of God's creation.

A key to this inner focus is the "Which Index." When you hear a statement that "no woman should be allowed to speak behind the pulpit," ask: Which? *Which* women? Should some men be prohibited? This "Which Index" can be useful for oneself, but also a useful question to use in small-group situations whenever you hear a didactic statement of indiscrimination.

4. Polarizing

Polarizing is the communication problem of placing elements in dichotomous (opposite) positions, refusing to accept that there could be gradations between the two poles. To illustrate, a frequent problem of polarizing is found in regard to what is meant by Christian perfection. Those conscientiously striving for heart perfection may erroneously believe that this must mean perfection in *all* areas of life. Thus if one who is extremely weary shouts at a child who brings a muddy puppy onto the freshly shampooed carpet, this indicates total spiritual failure. Polarizing is concluding there are only two positions:

PERFECTION   FAILURE

This is erroneous because there are all kinds of gradations in between perfection and abysmal failure.

This is true on all kinds of issues. Very few things are truly dichotomous, if examined. There are a few absolutes. One *is* male or female; one *is* redeemed or not; one *is* of a certain nationality or not. But in human actions, there are gradations in most things.

Haney gives two suggestions for correctives:

    a. Detect the contrary. In other words, discover if there is a middle ground. Contradictories (male or female) are dichotomous. Contraries, however, have gradations. In a polarized statement, look for the contraries. Every war has been engendered with polarized rhetoric: "We must go to war or become slaves," when, in many instances, there are all kinds of other options in middle ground. Sensitize yourself to looking for these. Few things are dichotomous.

    b. Specify the degree—apply the How-Much Index (e.g. religious/non-religious; believer/atheist; tall/short). . . . Ask for the "telling detail" of "how much." There are gradations between most things. When you ask "How much" to yourself or to group members, it helps you to pull back from the extreme position of a dichotomy. "Someone who would like to believe but has many doubts" is neither definitive of a believer or of an atheist. That "telling detail" is helpful in interpersonal understandings.[9]

5. Frozen Evaluation

This is "judgment set in concrete." This is viewing the world as remaining static, incapable of change. This is so common it is incredible . . . because it is so incredible to *not* be constantly aware of *change*.

I recently received a form requesting my evaluation

of a young woman applying for graduate school. She had been in many of my classes several years ago. She was a poor student. She never made above a C and made frequent *D*s. Though poorly motivated academically, she was the charm of the social campus world. Now I am asked to evaluate her possible performance in graduate school. How unfair if I write my impression of her as a young woman in her 20s more concerned with dating than rhetoric. She has *changed* in the intervening years. How? I do not know. But I refuse to give a "frozen evaluation" that she is *now* a poor risk for quality graduate work.

I remember back to my college days and realize the tremendous *change* that occurred in my motivation for study between college and graduate school. The only thing about human life (except for the absolutes such as the God/man relationship), that is *not* subject to change *is* change.

A major corrective in this communication barrier is the "When Index" which is a simple device to remind us to take *change* into account in all evaluations.[10]

6. Intensional Orientation

This is the communication barrier caused by a person wanting to center his concern and be guided by personal feelings rather than what is reality in life. He excludes observations, testimonials, or even facts.

One of the most tragic examples I have seen of this was a woman suffering with sugar diabetes who took some of the "whatsoever" scriptures and determined they should be answered in line with her "personal feelings." In group discussions, she would become irrational on this point so that we finally attempted to avoid the subject of God's ability to break natural law for His children. She became so intense in centering her concern on the belief that God would do that for her. In discussion, we tried to point out that God did not always answer with dramatic natural-law intervention. Paul was cited as a case in point.

But because she chose to let the "whatsoever" God-promises communicate to her what she personally desired, she ceased taking her insulin. She went into a diabetic coma and died.

Rarely will your small group experience the effect of communication problems as dramatic as this. But there is a constant pervasion in all discussion of persons, consciously or unconsciously, being guided by *personal feelings* rather than the *reality* of life. The small-group leader must work for the most commonsense, down-to-earth approach possible.

7. Blinders

This is a communication barrier that is named after the horse's blinders from another era. They kept the horse's view straight ahead and prevented distractions from either side. This is one of the greatest hindrances to learning discussion possible. We become so accustomed to looking at the Christian life in set, narrow, static ways that much of its dynamic creativeness is denied us.

A young man in one of our discussion groups presented the prayer request that he find a new job. When queried why, he said that his employer had decided to divide his job between two men. He felt it could not be done that way. We advised him to take off his "blinders" of how the job had always been done (within the strength levels of one man) and let his mind run free with the possibilities of how the job could be done in far-ranging outreach with the strength levels of two men. As a group, we came up with several job descriptions that so excited the young man and his employer that the new man was hired earlier than intended and the results are still amazing today. But had he kept his narrow view of what is, what has been, what must be, he could never have achieved this new level of fulfillment.

Recently I was planning a program which depended on the assistance of one man in the logistics of its execution. At the last minute, he told me he could not do the job. Trying to still my panic, I went to my office and said: "God, help me to *redeem* this unpleasant situation; tickets have been sold; advertising is out; help me to *use* this unhappy event for good." As I sat there striving to let my mind run free of all preconceived blinders of the problem, a solution came to me that was so ideal that it has transformed the quality and direction of the entire program.

Group leader, not only be very sensitive to this in your own personal life and in your life as a group leader, but strive to develop such an understanding in the lives of your group members. Encourage them to take off their "blinders" in unpleasant circumstances and look at the situation through the eyes of God who is creatively and dynamically at work.

Note that it is we who *put on the blinders* and stoically look through them. It is only when we deliberately work against them that we become most creative.

Haney's correctives are:

a. Talk with an outsider. (You will get an objective point of view from a person who, if he has blinders, at least has a different set.)

b. Kill "killer phrases." (Don't allow phrases like the man in my small group who used to come in with "It's always been done like this!" etc.)

c. Brainstorm with a group. (The illustration cited above clearly shows the value of this suggestion.)[11]

To these, a fourth may be added: Get alone with

103

God and ask Him to enable you to find creative ways to work through the problem.

8. Inference-Observation Confusion

This is a problem that arises when someone acts upon his inference *as if it were* an observation. This is probably the most insidious and yet most common of all communication problems.

I can look at a man and, by observation, state: "He is entering a church." I may just as confidently assert: "He is a member and regular attender of that church." But unless I actually have observed him in membership roles and in regular attendance, the latter is *a statement of inference.* I inferred he was an active part of the church because he was entering the building "as if he belonged there." He may be going in to apply for the job of caretaker. He may be going in to deliver a registered letter. He may be going in to make a date with the pastor's secretary. The point is that, since I have not observed his membership roles or his regular attendance, the latter statement for me has to be inference.

Observational and inferential statements are often extremely difficult to distinguish. Certainly the structure of our language offers no indication of their differences. There may be no grammatical, syntactical, orthographical, or punctuational or pronunciational distinctions between them whatsoever. Moreover, the tones or inflections in which they are uttered may sound equally "certain." . . .

In other words, there is nothing in the nature of our language . . . that makes it inescapable that we discriminate between inferential and observational statements. It seems reasonable to assume then, that our failure to distinguish on these *verbal* levels contributes appreciably to the difficulty we have on *nonverbal* levels, namely, our propensity to confuse inference and observation, per se. Thus, we find it

104

enticingly easy to make inferences and to utter inferential statements with the false assurance that we are dealing with "facts"—and the consequences of acting upon inferences *as if* they were observations are often less than pleasant.[12]

In one of my pastorates, a couple in the midst of marital strife had finally separated. A male friend of the wife knew how upset she was. He suggested that she spend that first night at the parsonage and he would stay at the house to be sure everything was all right.

The estranged husband drove by the house, saw the man's car in the driveway, *inferred what was happening,* and went to the next-door neighbors. Getting them out of bed, he had them follow him over to the house as he yelled: "Adultery! Adultery!" at the top of his lungs. There, they found the man awakening from sleep on the den sofa. He explained that the wife was at the parsonage; he was merely "protecting" the house with his presence.

A problem much less serious occurred in a small group. A new member attended for the first time with a little cap on her head that resembled the old Quaker caps. The gentleman who served the coffee did his job efficiently all evening—except that he completely ignored the young lady.

Finally, toward the end of the session when the atmosphere was quite relaxed, she asked if she could please have some coffee. Embarrassed, he said: "But if you're a Quaker..."

She was not a Quaker. The hat was a part of her college sorority's initiation.

She had been bewildered by the fact that she was not to be included in the group coffee drinking. She could have been truly hurt by it. The problem was that the gentleman *inferred* something that was not true.

105

Haney suggests that a helpful corrective for inference-observation confusion is to be *aware* of when one is inferring, as distinguished from observing, and then *calculating* the degree of probability that the inferences are correct.[13]

Confucius said: "To recognize what things you know, and what things you do not know—this is wisdom."

There are some times, of course, when we have to work with inferences; but we must constantly be aware that they *are* inferences, even if the degree of probability seems high.

9. Ambiguity

Ambiguity in a discussion can squelch a small group's purpose quickly. Be certain that all members' language is as clear and concise as possible. This is a prevalent communication breakdown in a mixed group of churched and unchurched. There is a lingo among church people based on their scriptural background, their pastor's sermons, etc., which the unchurched are not acquainted with. I can well remember the glazed look some of my group members got when one of my churchmen kept telling us his "ox was in the ditch." Since the man was a dignified banker who lived in a condominium, it was incongruous for these people to imagine he had an ox; and even if he had, what on earth would it be doing in what ditch? All biblically trained people understood the Old Testament image.

So constantly be on the alert to define terms completely and carefully. Always urge members to ask for clarification. The major key to effective communication in all group discussion is: "What do you mean?" Many are too shy to ask this, so the group leader must be on the alert to do it for them.

106

10. Stigma Words

Try to delete from your own vocabulary all words that tend to denigrate or ridicule. Encourage the same, as deftly as possible, within group members. Some such words are *hippie, radical, unchristian, childish, stupid, anti-American, ridiculous.* Labels as well as hostility-arousing and stigma words are divisive.

A young woman from a rural community joined one of our groups. This was in the 1950s when the name "cop" for policeman was not well accepted. All of us were a bit startled when this young lady would frequently, in the interchange of discussion, say to someone: "Oh, don't be a cop!" I could tell that a policeman member of the group was becoming more and more angry, and I struggled to find some way to handle the situation.

In dialogue with her, a group member said to the young woman: "Oh, you'll never understand!"

She again responded: "Don't be a cop!"

The policeman exploded. He jumped to his feet, his face red, his voice shaking: "I resent your constantly saying that."

She looked at him in amazement. "What do you mean? I wasn't even talking to you."

"But you were referring to me and my profession. I am a policeman."

Her eyes clouded with bewilderment. "So?"

It suddenly dawned on me that this was a communication breakdown, that there was some confusion of terms.

"Jackie, would you define the word 'cop'?" I asked.

Taken aback, she replied, "Why—a cop is—a person who cops out—who won't stick with a job until it's finished."

And, of course, the policeman and the entire group roared with relief and understanding. But her incorrect use of the "stigma word" would have created a difficult situation for the entire discussion purpose had she not been able to clarify its innocent connotation.

11. Cliches

The ability to think creatively, critically, free-wheelingly is halted when a member or members begin spouting truisms or pious platitudes. Thinking people are not interested in a discussion that is based on easy answers or fabled proverbs. Challenge your group to go beyond the hackneyed phrase; not that it may not be totally true, but that there might be fresh wording that would make it *new* and *real* to someone who had turned off the concept because of stale language.

12. Specificity

Usually little is accomplished in the discussion of generalities. One wants the most concrete example possible to be able to comprehend the point most fully. To illustrate, Gulley made this "ladder."

Things of Beauty
Decorative plants
Flowers
Roses
All white roses
A specific variety of white rose
The only white bloom on the first rosebush
just outside the front door.[14]

Now I can touch it; see it; examine it; understand.

My wife often says: "I understand theology best when I can see it lived." That is why the small-group leader is at his best when he presents the biblical concepts of the God/man relationship with the greatest degree of specificity possible. Jesus did that. He **didn't** just say: "God is love." He said: "God is like the loving earthly father who forgave his prodigal son." He gave us a specific that we could look at it, deal with it, examine it, and *understand* it.

Deep theological discussion is not your province as a small-group leader. The more specific, the more simple, the more concrete your language, the better your communication.

13. The Overtalkative Member

This is a problem in almost all groups. Some members will have to be dealt with privately, but try to avoid this, if possible. Some ways to try to get the message covertly to him is to specifically call for discussion from others by name. Another is to ask yes/no questions; and when this member answers, springboard from that to an open-ended question to another member. If he is dealing in abstractions, asking for specifics will often stop him in midstream. A leader-summary of "what we have agreed upon to this point" is always in order and can curtail a long-winded monologue.

One other tactic is to privately ask his help in bringing out the more hesitant members of the group. Ask him to relay questions he would normally answer to one of these persons, asking them to assist him in the answer. This enlistment of his help will often prove to *be* a help as well as solving the problem of his overcontributing.

14. Conflict

The leader should not allow himself to get entangled in a conflict. If one arises and needs to be quelled, the leader may interrupt to focus attention on the group process of learning. Conflict of ideas is a natural part of that. If everyone agreed, there would be no learning to be done. Each group member is an intelligent person whose opinions, stated calmly and rationally, are important. The more diverse the views, the wider will be the possibilities for finding a fresh understanding. If the group leader will handle conflict calmly, as a natural process of growing in a group, most of the "combatants" will respond in the same manner.

Many conflicts may be resolved by consulting a reference book. Others may be resolved with careful definition of terms. The most violent disagreement I have ever had in a small group was between two men who in their intensity had finally gotten to their feet. I asked them to define their key terms, which were *sin* and *mistake*. They sat down and tried the logical exercise of definition. And, to their amazement, they discovered that they actually were in doctrinal agreement when they sharpened their definition of terms.

The group leader must always keep in mind that "good discussion is born in conflict and thrives on conflict. But the conflict must be one of ideas rather than personalities."[15] This is where you must lay constant stress. If the group is to really explore ideas, to express questions and hang-ups, and to widen understanding, there are bound to be ideas that will be diverse. If everyone agrees on the same issues, then there is no growing edge to the group. Harnack and Fest acknowledge that: "Cooperative groups are obviously preferable to competitive groups, yet cooperation does not mean absence of conflict, as some believe. It does mean absence of conflict to block individuals and the vigorous presence of conflict to explore ideas."[16] If good humor and love can always prevail, the more combat of ideas, the healthier the conclusions in many cases.

There will not always be consensus. Members may agree to disagree. This, too, must be done with thinking, mature adults. One of my close friends, whom I admire as a Christian giant, has an interpretation of some scriptures that, with my experiential background, I could never accept. We smilingly agree to disagree. We still exchange our ideas on occasion, always broadening each other's scope, I believe. But I do not foresee the time when we will ever have consensus on this particular matter. But that isn't essential. Peter and Paul did not have consensus on all points either. The more important point is that we attempt to grow together in the dimensions God designed for us. And we do that best in community, in small-group discussion, even when we are not all of one and the same mind.

15. Getting Back on the Track

When group discussion has been drawn down some interesting side-path, the leader must bring things back to the focal center as quickly as possible because of time. Usually a restatement of the basic problem will readjust mental thought. If there is still interest in the marginal discussion, suggest that it be done during the fellowship time after the hour of structured Bible study is over. Your accepting of, and expressed appreciation for, the tangent question should be clear. Often the side-paths may be more uniquely needed in *this* group at *this* time than the structured curriculum. If you feel strongly this is the case, you may wish to let the evening be spent on the "side-path." But unless you feel this is the desire of most of the members, attempt to get back to the main focus and ask those interested in the other area to consider it later.

8

The Power of the Spirit

No matter how thoroughly one may study the techniques of group discussion, participation, and leadership, the small-group meeting will amount to little more than a neighborhood barbecue unless the Holy Spirit is present in a powerful way. Techniques, functions, tools, and organization all have their place, but it is a small place in relation to the presence of God's Spirit. Only He can make doubters into believers; only He can apply the Word of God to the human situation; only He can transform souls, lives, and circumstances.

"When the Holy Spirit, who is truth, comes, he shall guide you into all truth, for he will not be presenting his own ideas, but will be passing on to you what he has heard" (John 16:13, TLB).

We have spent a lot of time talking about the sensitivity of the small-group leader to various aspects of communication on the horizontal level. There must be a even greater emphasis placed upon the leader's sensitivity to communication on the vertical level. In many ways, in your small-group situation, you stand between God and man. And as God speaks to your heart vertically, and your heart openly articulates itself to your group members horizontally, you will find God's dialogue with men. What an awesome role for you!

No two people come to God by the same road. Few reach Him without stumbling, falling, hurting. There are seeds that grow a long time in darkness before they push up shoots into the sun. There are others that come to light at one thrust in a single day. As a group leader, working between God and man, you must deeply understand that the human soul meets barriers that it must cross to reach God. These barriers are unique in each situation. They are not always crossed at one stride.

The direction in which the soul travels is the important thing. The fact that someone is willing to join your small group to study God's Word indicates a reaching out toward God. Therefore, as you offer your hand to the ones who have already found God, so you must offer your hand to those who are still caught on the spikes of an infinite number of pains and anguishes. Therefore, the outward reach of your heart must be to serve God, but more, to be of service for God to others—your love for Him given freely to others. Love is that chameleon word that covers every person, in every condition, in every situation. God is love; and if you would be His representative to the members of your small group, your love must be also encompassing.

Pray deeply, personally, open-heartedly for each group member. Especially pray for those who do not personally please you. God will create a real change within you so that you develop a true understanding and affection for that person. It can work both ways, too. And it will not go unnoticed by all the others involved.

In the beginning, we stated that the *purpose* of the small group in the church was for *ministry;* for the fulfillment of the vertical/horizontal relationship. Vertically, together, you and your group members can *affirm* God. As you learn together of Him, you have a deeper sense of *who He is.* As you become more *unified in Him,* then the vertical stream flows in ever-widening dimension into the horizontal stream of brotherly love. The entire basis for interpersonal unity is the fact that *we are one in Jesus Christ himself.* Ours is a *shared* vertical relationship with the Father God; ours is a *shared* horizontal relationship with other brothers and sisters in the family of God. The *vertical* act of redemption is barren without the *horizontal* outreach to others.

Pray not only *for* your group members; pray *with* them. Often. Not only at the beginning and conclusion of a get-together session, but whenever there is a moment when God's assistance is needed. This open "practicing the presence of God" will not only bring His presence preciously near to each heart in the small group, it will set habit patterns for each to follow in their homes and personal lives.

I had a small-group leader one time who practiced this very well. When someone cried in a moment of heart-sharing, she would say: "I think we should pray now." And she promptly did so. When there was a conflict such as over the interpretation of a scripture, she would say: "I think we should pray now." And she promptly would do so. I remember my surprise, one time, when we were laughing heartily over something, and she paused to wipe her eyes in the fun and said: "I think we should pray now." And she promptly thanked God for the joy we shared with Him. I'll never forget that moment. How beautiful to share every detail of one's life with God!

114

Look throughout the membership of your church. Find people who have time (shut-ins, retired, etc.) to give to a prayer ministry. Take them a list of your group members. Write a brief resume of each. Take a picture of each group member if you can. Ask these saints to pray daily for these people. As your small group is enfolded daily, lovingly, by these unseen prayer partners, amazing things will begin to happen. You will find the presence of the Holy Spirit in more powerful dimension than you have ever experienced before. Do not try to assume your leadership responsibilities alone. Solicit as many prayer partners as possible. Keep them informed of the results of their prayers. Keep them actively involved in what is going on in the lives of "their people."

Footnotes

CHAPTER 1

1. William Newell, *Romans, Verse by Verse,* quoted in *How to Conduct Bible Classes,* by Albert J. Wallen (Wheaton: Scripture Press, 1969), p. 7.

CHAPTER 2

1. B. M. Bass, *Leadership, Psychology, and Organizational Behavior* (Evanston, Ill.: Harper and Row, 1960), p. 39.

2. Theodore Mills, *The Sociology of Small Groups* (New York: Prentice Hall, 1967), p. 2.

3. Paul A. Hare, *Handbook of Small Group Research* (New York: The Free Press, 1962), p. 5.

4. D. Cartwright and A. Zander, eds., *Group Dynamics: Research and Theory,* 2nd ed. (Evanston, Ill.: Row, Peterson, 1962).

5. G. C. Homans, *Social Behavior: Its Elementary Forms* (New York: Harcourt, Brace, 1961), p. 1.

6. R. M. Stogdill, "Personal Factors Associated with Leadership: A Survey of the Literature," *Journal of Psychology,* 25:18 (1948).

7. John K. Brilhart, *Effective Group Discussion* (Dubuque, Ia.: Wm. C. Brown, 1967), p. 12.

8. *Ibid.* (2nd ed.), pp. 30-32.

9. *Ibid.,* pp. 32-33.

CHAPTER 3

1. Irving Lee, *How to Talk with People* (New York: Harper and Row, 1952), Chap. 12.

2. George C. Homans, *The Human Group* (New York: Harcourt, Brace, 1950), p. 440.

3. Robert Tannenbaum, Irving R. Weschler, and Fred Massarik, *Leadership and Organization: a Behavioral Science Approach* (New York: McGraw Hill, 1961), p. 24.

4. Sol Levine, "An Approach to Constructive Leadership," *Journal of Social Issues* 5, no. 1 (1949): 46.

5. Stogdill, *Journal of Psychology* 25 (1948): 35.

6. Levine, *Journal of Social Issues* 5, no. 1 (1949): 48.

7. Tannenbaum et al., *Leadership and Organization,* p. 36.

8. David Berlo, *The Process of Communication* (New York: Holt, Rinehart, and Winston, 1960), p. 72.

9. Jane Blankenship, *Public Speaking: A Rhetorical Perspective* (Englewood Cliffs, N.J.: Prentice Hall, Inc., 1972), pp. 32-34.

CHAPTER 4

1. Halbert E. Gulley, *Discussion, Conference, and Group Process* (New York: Holt, Rinehart and Winston, 1968).

2. Norman Maier, *Problem-Solving Discussions and Conferences* (New York: McGraw Hill, 1963), pp. 171-77.

3. Lee, *How to Talk with People,* pp. 158-60.

CHAPTER 5

1. Brilhart, *Effective Group Discussion* (3rd ed.), pp. 142-43.

2. *Ibid.,* p. 114.

3. *Ibid.*

4. Lawrence Rosenfeld, "Nonverbal Communication in the Small Group," in *Small Group Communication: A Reader,* ed. Robert S. Cathcart and Larry Samovar (Dubuque, Ia.: Wm. C. Brown, 1964), p. 190.

5. *Ibid.,* p. 191.

6. *Ibid.*

7. R. Hung and Tip K. Lin, "Accuracy and Judgments of Personal Attributes from Speech," *Journal of Personality and Social Psychology,* VI (1966), p. 453.

8. Rosenfeld, "Human Interaction in the Small Group Setting, p. 198.

9. *Ibid.,* p. 199.

10. Albert Mehrabian, *Silent Messages* (Belmont, Calif.: Wadsworth Press, 1971), p. iii.

11. Edward Rintyre, "Three Useful Principles of Human Communication," *Small Group Communication,* p. 297.

12. Eliot D. Chapple, *Culture and Biological Man: Explorations in Behavioral Anthropology* (New York: Holt, Rinehart and Winston Publishers, 1970), p. vii.

13. Robert Tannenbaum, Irvin R. Weschler, and Fred Massarik, "The Process of Understanding People," *Interpersonal Dynamics: Essays and Readings of Human Interaction,* ed. Warren G. Bennis et al. (Homewood, Ill.: Richard Irwin, 1964), p. 732.

14. Rintyre in *Small Group Communication,* p. 299.

CHAPTER 6

1. Brilhart, *Effective Group Discussion* (2nd ed.), p. 26.

2. *Ibid.* (1st ed.), p. 17.

3. *Ibid.* (1st ed.), p. 18.

4. Thomas Gordon, *Group-centered Leadership: A Way of Releasing the Creative Power of Groups* (Boston: Houghton-Mifflin, 1955), pp. 181-82.

5. Brilhart, *Effective Group Discussion* (1st ed.), pp. 15-16.

6. Lewis Carroll (Charles Dodgson), *Alice's Adventures in Wonderland, Through the Looking Glass, and The Hunting of the Snark* (New York: The Modern Library, 1925), pp. 246-47.

7. Kenneth Burke, *A Rhetoric of Motives* (New York: Prentice-Hall, 1945), p. 55.

8. Bill Vaughn, "Billy Graham: A Rhetorical Study in Adaptation" (Ph.D. diss., University of Kansas), p. 47.

9. Ruth Vaughn, *The Man on the Center Cross* (Englewood, Colo.: Agape Drama Press, 1978), p. 18.

10. Joseph Luft, *Group Processes* (Palo Alto, Calif.: National Press Books, 1970), pp. 11-12.

11. *Ibid.,* p. 14.

12. *Ibid.*

13. C. S. Lewis, *The Case for Christianity* (New York: Macmillan, 1943); cited in Samuel Shoemaker, *And Thy Neighbor* (Waco, Tex.: Word Books, 1967), pp. 81-82.

14. Ruth Vaughn, "Please Care About Me." Unpublished book of poems, The University of Kansas.

15. Lawrence O. Richards, *69 Ways to Start a Study Group* (Grand Rapids: Zondervan Publishing House, 1973), pp. 71-73.

CHAPTER 7

1. See Blankenship, *Public Speaking,* p. 5.

2. *Ibid.,* pp. 7-8.

3. Carroll, *Alice's Adventures in Wonderland,* p. 246.

4. William F. Haney, *Communication and Organizational Behavior* (Homewood, Ill.: Richard Irwin, Inc., © 1973), p. 253.

5. *Ibid.,* p. 257.

6. *Ibid.,* pp. 270-74.

7. *Ibid.,* p. 309.

8. *Ibid.,* pp. 374-75.

9. *Ibid.,* p. 460.

10. *Ibid.,* p. 462.

11. *Ibid.,* p. 220.

12. *Ibid.*

13. *Ibid.*

14. Gulley, *Discussion Conferences* (2nd ed.), p. 125.

15. William S. Howell and Donald K. Smith, *Discussion* (New York: Macmillan Co., 1956), p. 256.

16. Victor Harnack and Thorrel B. Fest, *Group Discussion, Theory and Technique* (New York: Appleton-Century-Crofts, 1964), p. 176.